LOGOS LATIN

LOGOS LATIN

Julie Garfield

Illustrated by Mark Beauchamp

Moscow, Idaho

Published by Logos Press, a division of Canon Press
PO Box 8729, Moscow, ID 83843
800.488.2034 | www.logospressonline.com | www.canonpress.com

Julie Garfield, *Logos Latin 3: Student*
Copyright © 2013 by Julie Garfield

Illustrations by Mark Beauchamp
Copyright © 2013 by Logos Press??

Cover design by Lisa Beyeler
Interior design by Lisa Beyeler with Laura Storm
Interior layout by Laura Storm Design
Printed in the United States of America.

All rights reserved. No part of this publication may be reproduced, stored in a retrieval system, or transmitted in any form by any means, electronic, mechanical, photocopy, recording, or otherwise, without prior permission of the author, except as provided by USA copyright law.

Library of Congress Cataloging-in-Publication Data

[[forthcoming]]

13 14 15 16 17 18 19 20   10 9 8 7 6 5 4 3 2 1

Table of Contents

Introduction 11

Unit 1   13

List One 15
    Lesson One 19
    Lesson Two 23

List Two 29
    Lesson Three. 31
    Lesson Four 33
    Lesson Five 37
    Lesson Six 39

Unit One Review 41

Unit 2   45

List Three 47
    Lesson Seven. 49
    Lesson Eight. 55

List Four. 59
    Lesson Nine 63
    Lesson Ten. 67
    Lesson Eleven 71
    Lesson Twelve 75

Unit Two Review 79

Unit 3   83

List Five 85
    Lesson Thirteen 87
    Lesson Fourteen 91

List Six 95
    Lesson Fifteen 97
    Lesson Sixteen 101
    Lesson Seventeen 105
    Lesson Eighteen 109

Unit Three Review 113

Unit 4   119

List Seven 121
    Lesson Nineteen 123
    Lesson Twenty 127

List Eight 131
    Lesson Twenty-One 133
    Lesson Twenty-Two 139
    Lesson Twenty-Three 141
    Lesson Twenty-Four 143

Unit Four Review 147

Unit 5   153

List Nine 155
    Lesson Twenty-Five 159
    Lesson Twenty-Six 163

List Ten 167
    Lesson Twenty-Seven 169
    Lesson Twenty-Eight 173
    Lesson Twenty-Nine 177
    Lesson Thirty 181

Unit Five Review 185

Unit 6 — 189

List Eleven 191
    Lesson Thirty-One. 194
    Lesson Thirty-Two. 201

List Twelve 205
    Lesson Thirty-Three 207
    Lesson Thirty-Four 211
    Lesson Thirty-Five. 215
    Lesson Thirty-Six 217

Unit Six Review 221

Unit 7 — 227

List Thirteen 229
    Lesson Thirty-Seven 231
    Lesson Thirty-Eight 235

List Fourteen 239
    Lesson Thirty-Nine 243
    Lesson Forty. 247
    Lesson Forty-One 249
    Lesson Forty-Two 255

Unit Seven Review 259

Unit 8 — 265

List Fifteen 267
    Lesson Forty-Three 271
    Lesson Forty-Four 275

List Sixteen 279
    Lesson Forty-Five 281
    Lesson Forty-Six. 287
    Lesson Forty-Seven 291
    Lesson Forty-Eight. 293

Unit Eight Review 297

Unit 9   303

    Lesson Forty-Nine 305
    Lesson Fifty 311
    Lesson Fifty-One 319

Activity Pages   323

List One	Crossword Puzzle	325
List Two	Word Scramble	326
List Three	A Race Course	327
List Four	Comic Strip	328
List Five	Crossword Puzzle	329
List Six	Word Search	330
List Seven	A Winter Scene	331
List Eight	Macaronic Story	332
List Nine	Crossword Puzzle	333
List Ten	Word Search	334
List Eleven	Birds	335
List Twelve	Stained Glass Window	336
List Thirteen	Crossword Puzzle	337
List Fourteen	Word Search	338
List Fifteen	Story Problems	339
List Sixteen	Word Scramble	340

Reference Pages — 341

- **A Note About Chants** 343
- **Verb Chants** 344
- **Noun Chants** 346
- **Pronoun Chants** 348
- **Jingles and Nifty Saying** 351
- **Latin Verb Tense Chart I** 352
- **Latin Noun Endings Chart I** 353
- **Latin Verb Tense Chart II** 354
- **Latin Noun Endings Chart II** 355
- **Memory Work** 356
- **Visual Aid - Verb Stem Flowers** 360
- **Visual Aid - In a Nutshell** 362
- **Number Comparison Chart** 363

Glossary — 366

- **Latin to English** 366
- **English to Latin** 371

Index — 379

Introduction

Welcome to Logos Latin, Book 3

After traveling through *Logos Latin 1* and *Logos Latin 2*, you are ready for new challenges. You will encounter new Latin vocabulary words and review old ones. You will deepen and expand your understanding of Latin grammar. You will make connections between Latin and English that you didn't see before. You will build on the Latin foundation you already have, using familiar tools and acquiring some new tools as well.

You will learn a new verb family, the third conjugation, and you will discover how it differs from first and second conjugation verbs. You will also learn three new verb tenses, the perfect, pluperfect, and future perfect. You will learn how to do a verb synopsis, or verb summary, in all six verb tenses. You will build upon the third declension noun family you learned last year, adding some other third declension "cousins". You will dress up nouns by making adjectives agree with them, but with some new twists.

New in this book are sections on etymology, or word history. You will find your English dictionary a useful tool for discovering where some of our English words come from. How did a particular English derivative travel from ancient Rome to the United States of America? The word's etymology traces that journey and helps you build up your English vocabulary based on its Latin foundations. You will continue to do derivative digging as well, looking up the meanings of Latin derivatives.

Also new are some simplified Latin versions of *Aesop's Fables* which you will translate. Each unit will contain a fable which utilizes vocabulary and grammar learned in that unit. As in *Logos Latin 1* and *Logos Latin 2*, *Logos Latin 3* also contains activity pages which can be done in your spare time.

Building up your Latin knowledge becomes more challenging in *Logos Latin 3*. As with any building project, it is satisfying and rewarding to see the walls go up but hard work is required. Faithful, consistent study will yield good results if you follow the building plans in this book. I hope you will enjoy honing your Latin skills as you learn to use new tools in *Logos Latin 3*.

Julie Garfield

Unit 1

1 List One

VOCABULARY

Memorize the following Latin words and their translations.

WORD	DERIVATIVE	TRANSLATION
1. clāmō, -āre	_____	*shout*
2. exspoliō, -āre	_____	*rob*
3. iuvō, -āre	_____	*help*
4. narrō, -āre	_____	*tell*
5. ululō, -āre	_____	*howl*
6. dēvorō, -āre	_____	*swallow, devour*
7. properō, -āre	_____	*hurry, hasten*
8. cūrō, -āre	_____	*care for*
9. auscultō, -āre	_____	*listen to*
10. oppugnō, -āre	_____	*attack*
11. moneō, -ēre	_____	*warn*
12. rīdeō, -ēre	_____	*laugh, smile*
13. studeō, -ēre	_____	*study*

WORD	DERIVATIVE	TRANSLATION
14. terreō, -ēre	_____	*frighten*
15. Aesōpus, -ī, *m.*	_____	*Aesop*
16. Graecia, -ae, *f.*	_____	*Greece*
17. fābula, -ae, *f.*	_____	*story, fable*
18. vīcus, -ī, *m.*	_____	*village*
19. narrātor, narrātōris, *m.**	_____	*story teller*
20. nōn	_____	*not*

REVIEW WORDS

1. magister, magistrī, *m.*   *male teacher*
2. līberī, -ōrum   *children*
3. discipulus, -ī, *m.*   *boy student*
   (discipula, -ae, *f.*)   *(girl student)*
4. habitō, -āre   *live in, inhabit*
5. erat (linking verb)   *was*
6. et   *and*

* Third declension noun

List One

REVIEW CHANTS

PRESENT TENSE VERB ENDINGS

-ō — *I*	-mus — *we*
-s — *you*	-tis — *you all*
-t — *he, she, it*	-nt — *they*

FUTURE TENSE VERB ENDINGS

-bō — *I will*	-bimus — *we will*
-bis — *you will*	-bitis — *you all will*
-bit — *he, she, it will*	-bunt — *they will*

IMPERFECT TENSE VERB ENDINGS

-bam — *I was*	-bāmus — *we were*
-bās — *you were*	-bātis — *you all were*
-bat — *he, she, it was*	-bant — *they were*

FIRST DECLENSION NOUN ENDINGS

-a	-ae
-ae	-ārum
-ae	-īs
-am	-ās
-ā	-īs

SECOND DECLENSION NOUN ENDINGS

-us	-ī
-ī	-ōrum
-ō	-īs
-um	-ōs
-ō	-īs

List One

1 Lesson One

Definition of a *verb*:

A verb shows action or state of being.

A. VERB TENSE REVIEW

From memory, fill in the verb endings and their meanings below. Then use your chant charts to check your work.

PRESENT TENSE

Person	Singular	Plural
1st	-ō – *I*	
2nd		
3rd		

IMPERFECT TENSE

Person	Singular	Plural
1st	-bam – *I was*	
2nd		
3rd		

FUTURE TENSE

Person	Singular	Plural
1st	-bō – *I will*	
2nd		
3rd		

B. PERSON & NUMBER

Person refers to the person doing the action of a verb. *Number* refers to singular or plural. Using the charts above, fill in the correct **person** and **number** for the following verbs, and then provide the translation. You may abbreviate.

VERB	PERSON	NUMBER	TRANSLATION
1. terrēs	_____	_____	_____
2. rīdēbitis	_____	_____	_____
3. oppugnant	_____	_____	_____
4. cūrābō	_____	_____	_____
5. dēvorābāmus	_____	_____	_____
6. narrābat	_____	_____	_____
7. exspoliābunt	_____	_____	_____
8. clamābās	_____	_____	_____
9. iuvō	_____	_____	_____
10. monet	_____	_____	_____
11. properābimus	_____	_____	_____
12. auscultābātis	_____	_____	_____

C. VERB STEM REVIEW

The *stem* of a verb is that part of a verb to which endings are attached. (See Latin Flower Illustration in the reference section). To find the verb stem, remove the *-re* ending from the second principal part of the verb.

First Conjugation ("A" Family) example:

ululō, ululāre   Cross off the *-re* on *ululāre* and you have the verb stem, *ulula-*

Second Conjugation ("E" Family) example:

studeō, studēre   Cross off the *-re* on *studēre* and you have the verb stem, *stude-*

N.B. The stems of first conjugation verbs end in *-a*. The stems of second conjugation verbs end in *-e*.

D. PRACTICE

Write the stems of the verbs below. Then identify whether the verb is first conjugation or second conjugation.

VERB	STEM	CONJUGATION
1. rīdeō, rīdēre	_____	_____
2. auscultō, auscultāre	_____	_____

N.B. The *first person singular present tense*, for first conjugation verbs only, does not contain the entire verb stem. For example: The stem for *narrō, narrāre* is *narra-*, but the first person singular present tense, is *narrō*, not *narraō*.

E. DERIVATIVE DIGGING

A *derivative* is an English word that comes from another language, but we will focus on derivatives from Latin. As a review, fill in the blanks below about derivatives.

To be a derivative, the English word must have:

a similar _____ and

a similar _____ to the Latin word from which it comes!

Lesson One   21

Now choose one *derivative* from List 1, look up its meaning in an English dictionary, and write the definition on the lines.

Derivative: _____   Latin Origin: _____

Definition: _____

_____

_____

Lesson One

2 Lesson Two

Definition of a *noun*:
A noun names a person, place, or thing, and sometimes an idea.

A. NOUN REVIEW

In Latin, noun endings change depending on how the noun is used in a sentence. These endings are called *case* endings.

Write out the five noun cases from memory with the help of the "memory device" below.

NO_____

GENTLE_____

DAD_____

ACCUSES_____

APPLES_____

What case is used for subject nouns? _____

What case is used for direct objects? _____

B. NOUN DECLENSIONS

Just as verbs have families called *conjugations*, so nouns have families called *declensions*. Fill in the declension endings below from memory. Then check your spelling with the chant charts.

FIRST DECLENSION

-a	
-ae	

SECOND DECLENSION

-us	
-ī	

C. FINDING THE BASE OF A NOUN

In order to *decline* (put endings on) a noun, it is first necessary to find the base. To find the base, remove the ending from the *genitive* form of the noun. Two examples are given below.

NOMINATIVE	GENITIVE	BASE
fabula	fabulae	fabul-
vīcus	vīcī	vīc-

N.B. *Don't try to change the case*
Until you find the base.
The genitive case
Is the place to find the base!

Now decline these words in the boxes below.

fabula	
fabulae	

Lesson Two

vīcus	
vīcī	

D. TRANSLATION

<u>Underline</u> noun and verb endings, label parts of speech, and translate the following sentences. Many are Pattern 2* sentences.

1. Līberī magistrum auscultant. _____

2. Discipulī fābulās student. _____

    SN   LV   PrN
3. Aesōpus erat narrātor.** _____

4. Aesōpus Graeciam habitābat. _____

5. Iūlius et Claudius fābulam nōn auscultābant. _____

_____

6. Magister Iūlium et Claudium monet! _____

_____

7. Iūlia et Claudia rīdent. _____

* Pattern 2 sentences contain a subject noun and a direct object.
** Pattern 4 sentence.

Lesson Two

E. ETYMOLOGY

Etymology is defined in the dictionary as *the tracing of a word back as far as possible in its own language or to its source in earlier languages.* Most of our English words have made a journey, often traveling from ancient Rome, through France, across the channel to England, and finally sailing to America! Another way to express the idea of *etymology* is to refer to the history of a word. In this book, we will discover the *etymology* of some English derivatives from our Latin lists.

We will learn more about etymology in a future lesson, but for now, correctly spell the word *etymology* three times below:

_____

_____

_____

N.B. The *etymology* of a derivative is not the same as its *definition* (meaning).

2 List Two

VOCABULARY

Memorize the following Latin words and their translations.

WORD	DERIVATIVE	TRANSLATION
1. puer, -ī, *m.*	_____	*boy, child*
2. pastor, pastōris, *m.*	_____	*shepherd*
3. ovis, ovis, *f.*	_____	*sheep*
4. agnus, -ī, *m.*	_____	*lamb*
5. grex, gregis, *m.*	_____	*flock, herd*
6. lupus, -ī, *m.*	_____	*wolf*
7. labōrō, -āre	_____	*work*
8. vīcīnus, -ī, *m.*	_____	*male neighbor*
9. vīcīna, -ae, *f.*	_____	*female neighbor*
10. rūs, rūris, *n.*	_____	*the country*
11. mons, montis, *m.*	_____	*mountain*
12. lūdus, -ī, *m.*	_____	*school*
13. liber, librī, *m.*	_____	*book*

WORD	DERIVATIVE	TRANSLATION
14. iocus, -ī, *m.*	_____	*joke*
15. mendācium, -ī, *n.*	_____	*a lie, falsehood*
16. mendax, mendācis, *m.*	_____	*a liar*
17. vēritas, vēritātis, *f.*	_____	*truth*
18. culpō, -āre	_____	*blame*
19. iterum	_____	*again*
20. ad	_____	*to, toward, at (prep. w/ acc.)*

REVIEW WORDS

1. rogō, -āre — *ask*
2. spectō, -āre — *look at, watch*
3. nōn — *not*
4. sed — *but*
5. magister, -trī, *m.* — *male teacher*
6. magistra, -ae, *f.* — *female teacher*
7. puella, ae, *f.* — *girl*
8. habeō, -ēre — *have, hold*

List Two

3 Lesson Three

A. THIRD DECLENSION NOUNS

Highlight the nominative and accusative endings for the declensions below:

FIRST DECLENSION

-a	-ae
-ae	-ārum
-ae	-īs
-am	-ās
-ā	-īs

SECOND DECLENSION

-us	-ī
-ī	-ōrum
-ō	-īs
-um	-ōs
-ō	-īs

THIRD DECLENSION

-x	-ēs
-is	-um
-ī	-ibus
-em	-ēs
-e	-ibus

Third declension nouns are trickier to identify than first or second declension nouns. The *x* of nominative singular can stand for many different endings. In order to recognize third declension nouns, it is necessary to look at the *genitive singular ending*. Third declension nouns always have the ending *-is* in the genitive singular. Remember:

Don't try to change the case
Until you find the base.
The genitive case
Is the place to find the base!

Circle the correct case. In order to find the base of a noun, remove the ending from which case?

nominative   ablative   genitive

Practice finding the base of these third declension nouns. The first one is done as an example.

NOUN	BASE
1. grex, gregis	*greg-*
2. vēritas, vēritātis	_____
3. mons, montis	_____
4. pastor, pastōris	_____
5. ovis, ovis	_____
6. rūs, rūris	_____

B. PRACTICE
Decline the third declension noun *grex, gregis*. Be sure to find the base first!

	SINGULAR	PLURAL
NOM.	grex	
GEN.	gregis	
DAT.		
ACC.		
ABL.		

C. PRACTICE WITH THE ACCUSATIVE CASE
Write the accusative singular forms of the nouns below. Pay attention to the declension.

NOMINATIVE	ACCUSATIVE
1. mons	_____
2. grex	_____

Lesson Three

NOMINATIVE	ACCUSATIVE
3. lūdus	_____
4. ovis	_____
5. mendācium	_____
Challenge: rūs	_____

D. TRANSLATION

Label and translate these sentences.

1. Iūlius nōn labōrābat. _____

2. Magister Iūlium spectat et rogat, "Quid agis?"* _____
_____

3. Iūlius nōn vēritātem narrat. _____

4. Iūlius mendācium narrat: "Labōrō et librum studeō." _____
_____

5. Magister Iūlium culpat. _____

6. Iūlius magistrum narrat, "Mea culpa."** _____
_____

* What are you doing?
** My fault.

E. USING DERIVATIVES

Correctly use five derivatives from List 2 in a short paragraph. <u>Underline</u> the derivatives you use.

4 Lesson Four

A. GENITIVE OF POSSESSION

Highlight the genitive case endings in these declension charts.

FIRST DECLENSION

-a	-ae
-ae	-ārum
-ae	-īs
-am	-ās
-ā	-īs

SECOND DECLENSION

-us	-ī
-ī	-ōrum
-ō	-īs
-um	-ōs
-ō	-īs

THIRD DECLENSION

-x	-ēs
-is	-um
-ī	-ibus
-em	-ēs
-e	-ibus

Below are three reasons why the genitive case is so important in Latin.
1. The genitive singular is used to identify what *declension* a noun is from.
2. The genitive singular is used to find the *base* of the noun before adding the other case endings.
3. The genitive case shows *possession*.

In English, we show possession by using an apostrophe or by using the preposition *of*. Study the examples of both ways below:

Apostrophe	Prep. *of*
the (female) neighbor's lamb	the lamb of the (female) neighbor
Aesop's Fables	The Fables of Aesop
the shepherd's sheep	the sheep of the shepherd

Now look at the same examples in Latin that use the genitive case to show possession. Highlight the genitive endings.

agnus vīcīnae   *Fabulae Aesōpī*   *ōvis pastōris* or *oves pastōris**

* The word *sheep* can be singular or plural in English.

Lesson Four 33

Remember to put the apostrophe *after* the s for plural possessive nouns:
    greges pastorum   the shepherds' flocks

No apostrophe is needed when using the preposition "of" to show possession:
    greges pastorum   the flocks of the shepherds

N.B. In Latin, the possessive noun adjective often *follows* the noun it describes.

B. PRACTICE
Translate the following genitive phrases both ways.

PHRASE	APOSTROPHE	PREP. *OF*
1. mons lupōrum	_____	_____
2. grex vīcīnī	_____	_____
3. vīcus puellārum	_____	_____
4. lūdus magistrae	_____	_____
5. pastor gregis	_____	_____
Challenge: ōvis rūris	_____	_____

C. TRANSLATE: LATIN TO ENGLISH
Label and translate the sentences below.

1. Iūlia agnum habet. _____

_____

2. Lupus agnum Iūliae terrēbat. _____

34 Lesson Four

3. Lupi gregem pastōris oppugnābant. _____

4. Puer properābat ad vīcum et monēbat vīcum. _____

5. Iūlius et Claudius agnum Iūliae et ovēs pastōrum iuvābant. _____

D. TRANSLATE: ENGLISH TO LATIN
Label these sentences and translate into Latin.

1. Claudia was caring for the lamb of Julia. _____

2. The shepherd's boys frighten the wolves. _____

Challenge: The wolves of the country hurry to the mountain and howl.

_____

Lesson Four 35

E. ETYMOLOGY

You have learned that *etymology* is the history of a word. The dictionary uses abbreviations to show the languages a derivative has traveled through. Here are some abbreviations you may encounter as we look up the etymologies of derivatives:

> L. = Latin
> ML. = Middle Latin (used in the Middle Ages; also called *ecclesiastical* Latin)
> LL. = Late Latin
> VL. = Vulgur Latin (the Latin spoken by common people)
> Fr. = French
> It. = Italian
> G. = German
> Eng. = English

Sometimes, an *O* (which stands for *old*) may appear in front of another abbreviation. For example:

> OE = Old English
> OHG = Old High German

N.B. *Ecclesiastical* is a derivative of the Latin word *ecclesia*. Look up the word *ecclesia* in a Latin dictionary if you don't remember it. Where might Ecclesiasatical Latin be used?

_____

Lesson Four

5 Lesson Five

A. MAKING COMMANDS

To form a command in Latin, remove the *-re* ending from the *infinitive* of the verb. Remember, the infinitive is the second principal part of the verb. Study the example below.

1st Principal Part   **2nd Principal Part (Infinitive)**

oppugnō   oppugnāre   Oppugnā.
Oppugna lupum.   *Attack the wolf.*   (command to one person)

To make a plural command, add the ending *-te* to the singular command.

Oppugnā**te** lupum.   *Attack the wolf.*   (command to more than one person)

B. PRACTICE

Translate these commands into English and circle whether they are singular or plural.

1. Narrā vēritātem. _____ Singular / Plural

2. Monēte ovēs pastōris _____ Singular / Plural

3. Culpāte lupōs. _____ Singular / Plural

Now translate these commands into Latin.

4. Listen to the story. (singular command) _____

5. Hurry to the village. (plural command; Hint: you will need to use the proposition *ad*) _____

C. MORE PRACTICE
Using Lists 1 & 2, write three Latin commands. Take turns giving commands to your classmates.

1.

2.

3.

6 Lesson Six
The Boy Who Cried "Wolf"

Translate the fable below. Be sure to label parts of speech. Some words in the fable may be review or unfamiliar. Look in the Fable Glossary at the end of the lesson for help with those words.

1. Ōlim puer ovēs cūrābat. _____

2. Pastōrēs gregēs vigilābant. _____

3. Quandō lupī gregem pastōris oppugnābant, pastor vocābat, "Iuvā!" _____
_____

4. Puer iocōs amat et mendāciam narrat. _____

5. Puer simulat vidēre lupum. _____

6. Sed puer clamat, "Iuvā!" _____

7. Pastōrēs et vīcīnī properant ad puerum sed puer rīdet. _____
_____

8. Pastōrēs nōn lupum vident. _____

9. Pastōrēs nōn rīdent sed puerum monent. _____

10. Iterum puer clamat, "Iuvā!" et pastōrēs properant ad gregem puerī. _____
_____

11. Vīcīnī et pastōrēs puerum culpant sed puer rīdet. _____
_____

Lesson Six 39

12. Lupī gregem puerī oppugnant. _____

_____

13. Lupī puerum terrent et puer clamat, "Iuvā!" _____

_____

14. Pastōrēs et vīcīnī puerum auscultant et narrant,* "Puer vēritātem nōn narrat." _____

_____

15. Puerum nōn iuvant. _____

16. Lupī ovēs devorānt. _____

Morum praecepta:
Si puer mendacia semper narrat, tum nemo eī credet** quandō veritatem narrat.
(If a child always tells lies, then no one will believe him when he tells the truth.)

FABLE GLOSSARY

1. ōlim — *once (upon a time)*
2. vigilō, -āre — *guard, watch over*
3. simulō, -āre — *pretend*
4. videō, -ēre — *see*
5. quando — *when*

* We will learn this future form later.

Unit One Review

A. PRESENT STEM REVIEW

Underline the correct answer to these questions about the present tense verb stem and commands in Latin.

1. What principal part of the verb is used to find the present verb stem?   *first   second   third*

2. What ending is removed to find the present stem?   *-ne   -te   -re*

3. The present stem can also be used as: *a singular command   a question   an adverb*

4. What ending is used to form a plural command?   *-ne   -te   -re*

B. FIND THE VERB STEM

Fill in the blanks about verb stems and conjugations.

1. What is the stem of the verb *clamō, clamāre*? _____

2. What conjugation is it? _____

3. What is the stem of the verb *moneō, monēre*? _____

4. What conjugation is it? _____

C. TRANSLATE COMMANDS

Translate these commands into Latin.

1. Laugh. (singular command) _____

2. Laugh. (plural command) _____

3. Study the story. (singular command) _____

4. Study the story. (plural command) _____

D. TRANSLATE VERBS
Underline endings and translate the verbs below.

1. oppugnās   _____

2. auscultābāmus   _____

3. terrēbunt   _____

4. dēvorābam   _____

5. exspoliat   _____

6. properātis   _____

7. cūrābit   _____

8. iuvābō   _____

E. NOUN CASE REVIEW
Fill in the blanks about nouns.

1. What noun case is used for subject nouns? _____

2. What noun case is used for direct objects? _____

3. What noun case is used for possessive nouns? _____

4. What noun case is used to find the base of a noun? _____

5. What noun case tells which *declension* (noun family) a noun is from? _____

F. FIND THE BASE
Give the base for each of the nouns below.

1. mendax, mendācis _____

2. iocus, -ī _____

3. Graecia, -ae _____

4. narrātor, narrātōris _____

G. TRANSLATE
Label and translate the following sentences.

1. Pastor puerōs culpat. _____

2. Lupus ovem pastōris exspoliābat. _____

3. Līberī Fābulās Aesōpī studēbunt. _____

4. Iūlia mendācium nōn narrat. _____

5. Claudius et Iūlius properant ad lūdum vīcī. _____

Challenge: Vīcīnī mendācem narrant, "Vēritātem narrā!" _____

Unit One Review 43

H. PREPOSITION REVIEW

List as many derivatives as you can think of that begin with the preposition *ad*. One is done as an example. You may use an English dictionary for help.

admit, _____

_____

_____

I. MACARONIC FABLE

Write your own *macaronic* fable about the importance of telling the truth. Remember, you write a macaronic story in English, but where possible, substitute Latin words for the English. For this fable, choose words from Lists 1 and 2. You may add a moral to go with your fable.

Unit 2

3 List Three

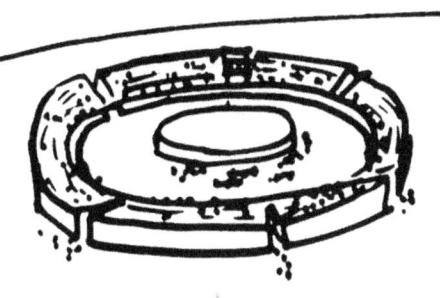

VOCABULARY

Memorize the following vocabulary words and their translations. Learn all four principal parts of verbs and the genitive singular and gender for nouns.

WORD	DERIVATIVE	TRANSLATION
1. cursor, cursōris, *m.*		*runner*
2. curriculum, -ī, *n.*		*a race, race course*
3. circus, -ī, *m.*		*an oval race course*
4. spatium, -ī, *n.*		*lap (in a race)*
5. delphīnus, -ī, *m.*		*dolphin*
6. arbiter, arbitrī, *m.*		*umpire, referee*
7. mēta, -ae, *f.*		*goal*
8. somnus, -ī, *m.*		*sleep*
9. brevis somnus		*a nap*
10. cunīculus, -ī *m.*		*rabbit*
11. praemium, -ī, *n.*		*reward, prize*
12. currō, currere, cucurrī, cursum		*run*
13. lūdō, lūdere, lūsī, lūsum		*play*

WORD	DERIVATIVE	TRANSLATION
14. exspectō, -āre, -āvī, -ātum	_____	*wait for, expect*
15. exerceō, -ēre, -uī, -itum	_____	*train, exercise*
16. contendō, -tendere, -tendī, -tentum	_____	*compete*
17. tardus, -a, -um	_____	*slow*
18. citus, -a, -um	_____	*fast, swift*
19. ē, ex (prep. w/abl.)	_____	*out of, from*
20. circum (prep. w/acc.)	_____	*around*

REVIEW WORDS

1. prīmus, -a, -um — *first*
2. secundus, -a, -um — *second*
3. tertius, -a, -um — *third*
4. apportō, -āre, -āvī, -ātum — *bring*
5. monstrō, -āre, -āvī, -ātum — *show, point out*
6. conciliō, -āre, -āvī, -ātum — *win*

List Three

7 Lesson Seven

A. THIRD CONJUGATION VERBS

So far, we have only dealt with verbs from the first and second conjugations. First conjugation verbs are sometimes called the "A" Family because the verb stem ends in *-a,* and that vowel appears before the verb endings (with the exception of the first person singular). Second conjugation verbs can be referred to as the "E" Family because the verb stem ends in an *-e* which appears before all verb endings. Study the conjugated examples below and highlight the verb endings.

FIRST CONJUGATION

Present Tense

amō	amāmus
amās	amātis
amat	amant

Imperfect Tense

amābam	amābāmus
amābās	amābātis
amābat	amābant

Future Tense

amābō	amābimus
amābis	amābitis
amābit	amābunt

SECOND CONJUGATION

Present Tense

videō	vidēmus
vidēs	vidētis
videt	vident

Imperfect Tense

vidēbam	vidēbāmus
vidēbās	vidēbātis
vidēbat	vidēbant

Future Tense

vidēbō	vidēbimus
vidēbis	vidēbitis
vidēbit	vidēbunt

Notice that the verb endings are *identical* for both conjugations. *Amō* and *video* are the verbs that we regularly chant as examples of these conjugations or verb families.

Now we will learn a new verb family that acts somewhat differently. It is called *third conjugation*. We will use the third conjugation verb *duco*, which means "lead," as our example. The endings on the third conjugation examples appear in bold type. Highlight these endings and pay attention to how they differ from endings for the first and second conjugations.

THIRD CONJUGATION

Present Tense

dūcō	dūc**imus**
dūc**is**	dūc**itis**
dūc**it**	dūc**unt**

Imperfect Tense

dūcēbam	dūcēbāmus
dūcēbās	dūcēbātis
dūcēbat	dūcēbant

Future Tense

dūc**am**	dūc**ēmus**
dūc**ēs**	dūc**ētis**
dūc**et**	dūc**ent**

Which third conjugation verb tense looks the *most* different from the endings we learned for first and second conjugations? Even though the endings look different in third conjugation, the meanings remain the same. Let's compare the third person singular verb forms from each conjugation.

PRESENT TENSE

First Conjugation: ama**t** - *he, she, it loves*
Second Conjugation: vide**t** - *he, she, it sees*
Third Conjugation: dūc**it** - *he, she, it leads*

IMPERFECT TENSE
    First Conjugation: amā**bat** - *he, she, it was loving*
    Second Conjugation: vidē**bat** - *he, she, it was seeing*
    Third Conjugation: dūcē**bat** - *he, she, it was leading*

FUTURE TENSE
    First Conjugation: amā**bit** - *he, she, it will love*
    Second Conjugation: vidē**bit** - *he, she, it will see*
    Third Conjugation: dūc**et** - *he, she, it will lead*

B. PRACTICE

Practice translating forms of the third conjugation verbs below. Highlight endings. The first two are done as examples.

1. curr**unt**   *they run, they are running, they do run*

2. curr**ēmus**   *we will run*

3. ludit _____

4. contendēbant _____

5. ludēs _____

6. contenditis _____

7. currēbāmus _____

8. lūdunt _____

9. lūdent _____

10. lūdēbant _____

Lesson Seven 51

C. IDENTIFYING VERB CONJUGATIONS

To identify a verb conjugation, it is necessary to find the clues in the first two principal parts of the verb. Compare and contrast the first two parts of our "conjugation representatives" below.

	1st Part	2nd Part
First Conjugation	amō	amāre
Second Conjugation	videō	vidēre
Third Conjugation	dūcō	dūcere

Notice that first conjugation verbs have a "lonely" -o with no other vowel in front of it in the first part, while the second part ends in -āre.

Second conjugation verbs are easy to recognize because they have an -e before the -o in the first part, and an -ēre in the second part. Also notice the macron over the -ē.

Third conjugation verbs combine elements of both. The first part looks like first conjugation's "lonely" -o, but the second principal part acts like second conjugation. Someone once suggested that this is like a math equation, and you can use this method to help you remember how to recognize third conjugation. *Dūcō* will be our third conjugation example:

    dūcō   dūcere
    1 (first conjugation) + 2 (second conjugation) = 3 (third conjugation)

Using the information from above, identify the verb conjugations below:

VERB   **CONJUGATION**

1. currō, currere _____

2. exerceō, exercēre _____

3. exspectō, exspectāre _____

4. lūdō, lūdere _____

D. FINDING THE PRESENT STEM FOR THIRD CONJUGATION VERBS

To find the stem of a third conjugation verb, remove the *-o* from the *first* principal part of the verb. For example:

        1ˢᵗ Principal Part   Present Stem
            dūcō   *dūc-*

Write the present stem for the third conjugation verbs from List 3 on the blanks.

1. currō _____

2. lūdō _____

3. contendō _____

E. DERIVATIVE DIGGING

Look up the English derivative *arbitrate* and write its definition.

arbitrate: _____

_____

From what Latin word does it come?

Latin origin: _____

Lesson Seven

8 Lesson Eight

A. MORE PRACTICE WITH THIRD CONJUGATION

Using your third conjugation verb chart, underline endings and then translate these verbs. All are from the *present, imperfect,* and *future.*

1. lūdit _____

2. lūdet _____

3. lūdēbat _____

4. currēbāmus _____

5. currēmus _____

6. currimus _____

7. contenditis _____

8. contendēbātis _____

9. contendētis _____

10. curram _____

11. lūdō _____

12. contendēbam _____

B. PRACTICE

Underline endings, identify the conjugation, and translate verbs from *first, second,* and *third* conjugations. Refer to your verb charts if you are unsure.

VERB	TRANSLATION	CONJUGATION
1. exspectābimus	_____	_____
2. lūdēmus	_____	_____
3. exercēbat	_____	_____
4. exspectant	_____	_____
5. contendunt	_____	_____
6. curris	_____	_____

Challenge words:

7. current	_____	_____
8. exercent	_____	_____

C. TRANSLATION

Label and translate these sentences:

1. Iūlius, Claudius, et discipulī contendent. _____

_____

2. Cursōrēs exercent et spatia currunt circum curriculum. _____

_____

Lesson Eight

3. Delphīnī* spatia monstrant. _____

_____

4. Iūlia cunīculum apportat ad curriculum. _____

_____

5. Claudia et Iūlia cursōrēs spectābant sed cunīculum nōn spectābant. _____

_____

6. Cunīculus Iūliae properat ad cursōrēs. _____

_____

7. Claudius currit ad mētam et praemium secundum conciliat. _____

_____

8. Claudius Iūlium exspectābat ad mētam. _____

_____

9. Iūlius praemium tertium conciliat. _____

_____

10. Sed cunīculus Iūliae praemium prīmum conciliat! _____

_____

* Stone dolphins or eggs were used to mark laps in chariot races.

D. ETYMOLOGY

Study this example of an etymology for the English derivative *dolphin*. Notice that the etymology appears in brackets [ ].

[ME. *dolfin*< OFr. *dalphin* <VL. *dalfinus*, for L. *delphinus*< Gr. *delphinos*]

The symbol < means *comes from*. Thus the etymology above could be read like this: "The English word *dolphin* comes from the Old French *dalphin*, which comes from Vulgar Latin *dalfinus*, for the Latin *delphinus*, which comes from the Greek *delphinos*."

 # List Four

VOCABULARY

Memorize the following vocabulary words and their translations. Learn all four principal parts of verbs and the genitive singular and gender for nouns.

WORD	DERIVATIVE	TRANSLATION
1. lepus, leporis, *m.*	_____	*hare*
2. testūdo, testūdinis, *f.*	_____	*turtle, tortoise*
3. testa, -ae, *f.*	_____	*shell*
4. arbor, arboris, *f.*	_____	*tree*
5. via, viae, *f.*	_____	*road, way*
6. victor, victōris, *m.*	_____	*winner, victor*
7. auris, auris, *f.*	_____	*ear*
8. vulpēs, vulpis, *f.*	_____	*fox*
9. excitō, -āre, -āvī, -ātum	_____	*wake*
10. turgeō, -ēre, tursī, ——	_____	*swell up*
11. ambulō, -āre, -āvī, -ātum	_____	*walk*

WORD	DERIVATIVE	TRANSLATION
12. tardō, -āre, -āvī, -ātum	_____	*slow down, delay*
13. volō, -āre, -āvī, -ātum	_____	*fly*
14. ūtor*	_____	*use*
15. longus, -a, -um	_____	*long*
16. stultus, -a, -um	_____	*foolish*
17. superbus, -a, -um	_____	*proud*
18. dēfessus, -a, -um	_____	*tired, weary*
19. sub (prep. w/abl.)	_____	*under*
20. in (prep. w/abl.)	_____	*in, on*

* *Ūtor:* This word always takes the ablative.

When *ūtor* is conjugated in the present tense, it looks like this:

ūtor – *I use*	ūtimur – *we use*
ūteris – *you use*	ūtiminī – *you all use*
ūtitur – *he, she, it uses*	ūtuntur – *they use*

When paired with the ablative form of *brevis somnus,* the phrase means *to take a nap.*
    Brevī somnō ūtor = *I take a nap.*
    Brevī somnō ūteris = *You take a nap.*
    Brevī somnō ūtitur = *He takes a nap.*

List Four

REVIEW WORDS

1. properō, -āre, -āvī, -ātum — *hurry, hasten*
2. habeō, -ēre, -uī, -itum — *have, hold*
3. praemium, -ī, *n.* — *prize*
4. videō, -ēre, vīdī, vīsum — *see*
5. malus, -a, -um — *wicked, bad, evil*
6. est — *he, she, it is*
7. sed — *but*
8. domus, ūs, *f.* — *home*
9. dō, dāre, dedī, datum — *give*
10. monstrō, -āre, -avī, -ātum — *show, point out*
11. ad (prep. w/acc.) — *to, toward, at*

9 Lesson Nine

A. ADJECTIVE REVIEW

Adjectives must match the nouns they describe in three ways.

GENDER: Gender refers to whether a noun is masculine, feminine, or neuter. Gender in Latin is not limited to people or animals. In Latin, a thing can often be masculine or feminine. In English, things are almost always neuter, that is neither masculine nor feminine.

NUMBER: Number refers to whether a noun is singular or plural. If the noun is singular, then the adjective describing it must be singular. If the noun is plural, the adjective describing it must be plural.

CASE: If a noun is in the nominative case, then the adjective must also be nominative. This is true for all five noun cases. Study the summary of noun-adjective agreement below:

1. Gender
    - Masculine (*-us*): Use the second declension endings when describing masculine nouns.
    - Feminine (*-a*): Use first declension endings when describing feminine nouns.
    - Neuter (*-um*): Use second declension neuter endings when describing neuter nouns.

2. Number
    - Singular
    - Plural

3. Case
    - Nominative
    - Genitive
    - Dative
    - Accusative
    - Ablative

N.B. Adjectives do *not* have to match the noun in *declension*.

B. TRANSLATION: LATIN TO ENGLISH
Label and translate the sentences below into English.

1. Cunīculus superbus Iūliae praemium prīmum conciliābat. _____

2. Cunīculus stultus brevī somnō ūtitur* sub arbore. _____

3. Vulpēs mala cunīculum stultum videt. _____

4. Vulpēs ambulat ad cunīculum dēfessum. _____

5. Cunīculus habet aurēs longās sed vulpem nōn auscultat. _____

6. Lepus citus cunīculum stultum excitat. _____

7. Vulpēs mala currit in arboribus. _____

C. TRANSLATION: ENGLISH TO LATIN
Label these English sentences and translate them into Latin.

1. Julia, Claudia, and the girl students run around the race course. _____

* *Takes a nap.*

Lesson Nine

2. Julia wins first prize. _____

_____

3. Tired Julia walks toward home and she takes a nap. _____

_____

Challenge: The swift girls fly around the long oval race course. _____

_____

D. DERIVATIVE DIGGING
Correctly use at least five derivatives from List 4 in a short paragraph. Underline the derivatives.

_____

_____

_____

_____

_____

_____

_____

_____

_____

Lesson Nine

10 Lesson Ten

A. DATIVE CASE REVIEW

We have been translating Pattern 2 sentences containing subject nouns, verbs, and direct objects. Now we will translate Pattern 3 sentences which contain *indirect objects*. In Latin, indirect objects go in the dative case. Consider the examples below.

>   SN   V-t   IO   Adj   DO
> The referee gives Claudius second prize.

Now compare the sentence above to the Latin version:

>   SN   IO   DO   Adj   V-t
> Arbiter Claudiō praemium secundum dat.

The dative case can also be translated with the prepositions *to* or *for*. For the sentence above we could say:

>   SN   V-t   Adj   DO   P   OP
> The referee gives second prize *to* Claudius.

Notice how this affects the labeling. In this instance, the dative case is translated by using the preposition *to* and an object of preposition.

B. PRACTICE

Practice labeling and translating Pattern 3 sentences containing the dative case below. Do not use *to* or *for*. Hint: Each sentence also contains a possessive noun.

1. Iūlius Saxō testam testūdinis monstrat. _____

_____

2. Iūlius Iūliae testam testudinis dat. _____

_____

3. Iūlia amīcīs testam testūdinis monstrābit._____

_____

Now translate the sentences above using either the preposition *to* or *for* instead of an indirect object:

1. _____

2. _____

3. _____

C. LINKING VERB REVIEW
Fill in the present tense meanings of the linking verb in the box below.

LINKING VERB (PRESENT TENSE)

sum —	sumus —
es —	estis —
est —	sunt —

Sentences that contain linking verbs can be called Pattern 4 sentences. In Pattern 4 sentences, the linking verb can be followed by a *predicate noun*. The predicate noun renames the subject noun. Consider the example below:

      SN   LV   PrN
    Julius is the winner.

Does *winner* mean the same thing as *Julius*?
If the answer is yes, then *winner* is a predicate noun.

Now look at a Pattern 2 example:

     SN   V-t   DO
   Julius watches the winner.

Does *winner* mean the same thing as *Julius*?
No, *Julius* and the *winner* are two different people.

Look at the same sentences in Latin:

```
          SN    LV    PrN
        Iūlius  est  victor.
```
Victor is in the nominative case.
Predicate nouns always go in the nominative case.
Think of this as an addition problem: 2 + 2 = 4
   "4" is another way of saying 2 + 2
   Victor is another way of saying *Iūlius*.

Now look at the Pattern 2 example in Latin:
```
          SN     DO      V-t
        Iūlius  victōrem  spectat.
```
Direct objects always go in the accusative case.

N.B. Study this negative example of a Pattern 4 sentence (using the adverb *not*):
   Iūlius nōn est victor can be translated as *Julius is not the winner.*

D. TRANSLATION

Translate the pairs of sentences below and note whether they are Pattern 2 (SN - V-t - DO) or Pattern 4 (SN-LV-PrN).

PATTERN

1. Claudius puerum excitat. _____ _____

   Claudius est puer. _____ _____

2. Claudius et Iūlius sunt puerī. _____ _____

   Claudius et Iūlius puerōs tardant. _____ _____

3. Iūlia est puella. _____ _____

   Iūlia puellam exspectat. _____ _____

4. Vulpēs lepōrem culpat. _____ _____

   Vulpēs nōn est lepus. _____ _____

E. ETYMOLOGY
Study the etymology of the English derivative *volley*.

[MFr. *volee* < VL. *volata* < fem. of L. *volatus*, pp. of *volare*, to fly]

Write out this etymology with the help of your teacher on the lines below.

_____

_____

_____

_____

_____

_____

11 Lesson Eleven

A. REVIEW FIRST, SECOND, & THIRD CONJUGATION

Fill in the present, imperfect, and future tense endings and meanings in the charts below. Remember, first and second conjugations ("A" Family and "E" Family) use the same endings, but the third conjugation has its own endings.

FIRST & SECOND CONJUGATIONS

PRESENT TENSE

-ō – I	

IMPERFECT TENSE

-bam – I was	

FUTURE TENSE

-bo – I will	

THIRD CONJUGATION

PRESENT TENSE

-ō – I	

IMPERFECT TENSE

-ēbam – I was	

FUTURE TENSE

-am – I will	

Identify the conjugations of the verbs below by referring to the first two principal parts of the verbs on Lists 3 and 4. Then translate the verbs.

VERB	CONJUGATION	TRANSLATION
1. currit	_____	_____
2. tardābit	_____	_____
3. turget	_____	_____
4. contendet	_____	_____

B. TRANSLATE NOUN-ADJECTIVE PHRASES

Translate these noun-adjective phrases into Latin. Remember, adjectives must match the noun they describe in gender, number, and case. Use the case indicated.

1. the proud hare (nominative) _____

2. the long roads (accusative) _____

3. the foolish fox (dative) _____

4. the fast dolphins (nominative) _____

C. NOUN CASE REVIEW

Match the noun cases to the correct parts of speech by drawing lines between them.

Nominative   Object of the Preposition

Genitive   Indirect Object

Dative   Subject Noun

Accusative   Possessive Noun

Ablative   Direct Object

Now translate this Pattern 3 sentence (SN, V-t, DO, IO).

Claudius Iūlio delphīnum monstrābat. _____

_____

12 Lesson Twelve
The Tortoise & the Hare

Translate the fable of *The Tortoise and the Hare*. You do not have to label unless you are having difficulty on a particular sentence. In that case, labeling may help.

1. Lepus citus potest currere. _____

2. Testūdo nōn potest currere. _____
_____

3. Lepus habet aurēs longās. _____

4. Testūdo testam dūram habet. _____

5. Lepus est citus sed testūdo est tarda. _____
_____

6. Lepus superbus testūdinem tardam rīdet. _____
_____

7. Lepus et testūdo contendunt in curriculō. _____
_____

8. Lepus testam testūdinis rīdet et spatia currit circum testūdinem. _____
_____

9. Vulpēs est arbiter. _____
_____

Lesson Twelve   75

10. Lepus citus in viā longā currit. _____

11. Testūdo tarda nōn currit sed ambulat in viā. _____
_____

12. Lepus testūdinem nōn potest vidēre. _____
_____

13. Lepus lūdit et *brevī somnō utitur* sub arbōre. _____
_____

14. Testūdo ambulat ad mētam. _____

15. Lepus dēfessus excitat et currit ad mētam. _____
_____

16. Testūdo exspectat ad mētam. _____

17. Vulpēs testūdini praemium dat. _____
_____

18. Testūdo est victor! _____

Morum praecepta: Lente et firme curriculum vincit. *(Slow and steady wins the race)*

Lesson Twelve

FABLE GLOSSARY

1. potest — *he is able*
2. dūrus, -a, -um — *hard*
3. rīdeō, -ēre, rīsī, risum — *laugh at*

Draw an illustration of the fable. Label any pictures of words from Lists 3 and 4 in Latin.

Unit Two Review

A. CONJUGATION REVIEW
Identify the conjugation of the verbs below.

VERB   **CONJUGATION**

1. exerceō, exercēre _____

2. lūdō, lūdere _____

3. exspectō, exspectāre _____

4. tardō, tardāre _____

5. currō, currere _____

6. turgeō, turgēre _____

B. VERB TRANSLATION
Translate the following verbs.

VERB	TRANSLATION	TENSE
1. contendet	_____	_____
2. contendit	_____	_____
3. turget	_____	_____
4. ambulābimus	_____	_____
5. lūdimus	_____	_____

VERB	TRANSLATION	TENSE
6. lūdēmus	_____	_____
7. lūdēbāmus	_____	_____
8. excitat	_____	_____
9. tardābō	_____	_____
10. curram	_____	_____

C. NOUN-ADJECTIVE AGREEMENT

Answer the following questions about noun-adjective agreement.

1. What are the three genders? _____, _____, _____

2. Give the gender of these adjective endings.

-us _____

-a _____

-um _____

3. What is meant by *number*? _____ or _____

4. Write out the five noun cases in order.

_____

_____

_____

_____

_____

5. Which case is used for subject nouns?_____

6. Which case is used for direct objects?_____

7. Which case is used for possessive nouns?_____

8. Which case is used for indirect objects?_____

D. ADJECTIVE PRACTICE
In each sentence below, underline the correct form of the adjective and then translate the sentences. Adjectives are *italicized*.

1. Lepus *citus/cita/citum* aurēs *longās/longōs* habet. _____

2. Arbiter *superbus/superba* testūdinī *tardae* praemium *prīmum* dat. _____

Challenge sentence: Cunīculī *stultae/stultī* currunt circum *longum/longam*. _____

E. PATTERN 3 PRACTICE
Label and translate these Pattern 3 sentences (SN, V-t, IO, DO).

1. Iūlius Claudiō leporem monstrābat. _____

2. Arbiter victōrī praemium dabit. _____

3. Iūlia Claudiae viam longam monstrat. _____

F. PATTERN 4 PRACTICE
Label and translate these Pattern 4 sentences (SN, LV, PrN).

1. Testūdo est victor. _____

2. Lepus nōn est victor. _____

3. Claudius et Iūlius sunt cursōres. _____

G. COMPOUND SENTENCE TRANSLATION
Label and translate these compound sentences.

1. Puellae spatia currunt, sed nōn contendunt. _____
_____

2. Testūdo ambulābat ad mētam sed nōn brevī somnō ūtitur. _____
_____

H. DERIVATIVE PRACTICE
Use at least five derivatives from Lists 3 and 4 in a short paragraph.

_____
_____
_____
_____
_____
_____

Unit 3

5 List Five

VOCABULARY

Memorize the following vocabulary words and their translations. Learn all four principal parts of verbs and the genitive and gender for nouns.

WORD	DERIVATIVE	TRANSLATION
1. cibus, -ī, *m.*	_____	*food*
2. cēna, -ae, *f.*	_____	*dinner, meal*
3. prandium, -ī, *n.*	_____	*lunch*
4. cāseus, -ī, *m.*	_____	*cheese*
5. nux, nucis, *f.*	_____	*nut*
6. glans, glandis, *f.*	_____	*acorn*
7. frūmentum, -ī, *n.*	_____	*grain*
8. mālum, -ī, *n.*	_____	*apple*
9. autumnus, -ī, *m.*	_____	*autumn*
10. aestas, aestātis, *f.*	_____	*summer*
11. coquus, -ī, *m.**	_____	*a cook*
12. epulae, -ārum, *f.*	_____	*feast*

* coqua, -ae, *f.*, female cook

WORD	DERIVATIVE	TRANSLATION
13. mensa secunda, -ae, *f.*	_____	*dessert*
14. epistula, -ae, *f.*	_____	*letter*
15. rurī	_____	*in the country*
16. edō, -ere, ēdī, ēsum	_____	*eat*
17. scrībo, -ere, scrīpsī, scrīptum	_____	*write*
18. legō, -ere, lēgī, lectum	_____	*read*
19. carpō, -ere, carpsī, carptum	_____	*pluck, pick*
20. multus, -a, -um	_____	*much, many*

REVIEW WORDS

1. bāca, -ae, *f.* *berry*
2. pōmum, -ī, *n.* *fruit*
3. currō, -ere, cucurrī, cursum *run*
4. dēvorō, -āre, -āvī, -ātum *swallow*
5. invītō, -āre, -āvī, -ātum *invite*
6. amīcus, -ī., *m.* *friend*
7. vīnum, -ī, *n.* *wine*
8. habeō, -ere, -uī, -itum *have, hold*
9. properō, -āre, -āvī, -ātum *hurry, hasten*
10. moneō, -ēre, -uī, -itum *warn*
11. imperō, -āre, -āvī, -ātum *order*
12. oppugnō, -āre, -āvī, -ātum *attack*
13. apportō, -āre, -āvī, -ātum *bring*
14. studeō, -ēre, -uī, —— *study*
15. labōrō, -āre, -āvī, -ātum *work*
16. exspectō, -āre, -āvī, -ātum *wait for*
17. lupus, -ī, *m.* *wolf*
18. liber, -brī, *m.* *book*
19. ē, ex (prep. w/abl) *out of, from*

List Five

13 Lesson Thirteen

A. PRESENT VERB STEM REVIEW

For first and second conjugation verbs, the present stem is found by removing the ending from which principal part? Using the first conjugation verb *amō*, circle the correct answer.

1st	2nd	3rd	4th
amō	amāre	amāvī	amātum

You should have circled *amāre*.

What is another name for the second part of the verb? _____

What does the *-re* mean on the end of the second principal part? _____

What does *amāre* mean? _____

After removing the *-re* ending from the second principal part of the verb, we are left with the *present stem*.

What is the present stem for *amō, amāre*? _____

We can add present, imperfect, and future tense verb endings to the present stem. Consider this "Latin flower." We will use the stem of *amō, amāre* as our example.

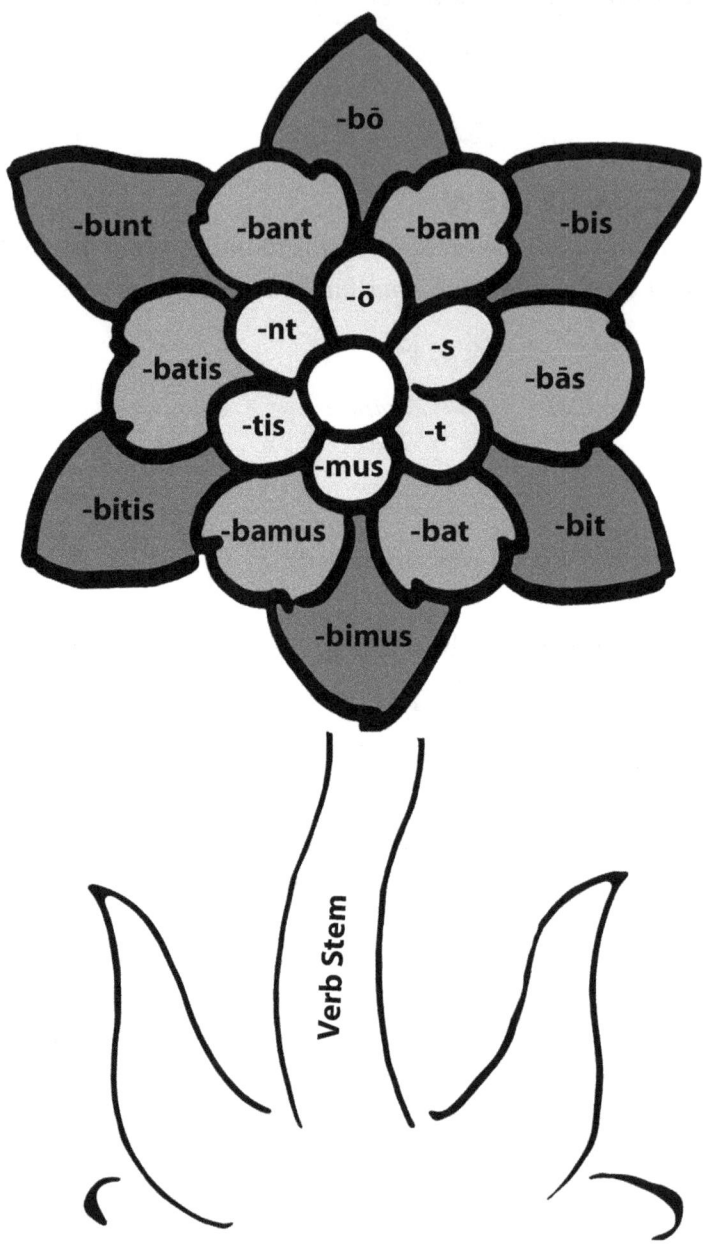

Lesson Thirteen

Now write the present stems of some other first and second conjugation verbs.

1. habeō, habēre _____

2. dēvorō, dēvorāre _____

3. invītō, invītāre _____

4. moneō, monēre _____

B. COMMANDS

The present stem has another important use; it can be a singular command (command to one person). Consider the examples below.

Habē cēnam.	*Have dinner.*
Dēvorā cāseum.	*Swallow the cheese.*
Invītā Claudiam.	*Invite Claudia.*
Monē Iūlium.	*Warn Julius.*

Who is always the implied subject of a command? _____

To form a plural command, add *-te* to the present stem.

Līberī, habēte cēnam.	*Children, have dinner.*
Puerī, dēvorāte cāseum.	*Boys, swallow the cheese.*
Puellae, invītāte Claudiam.	*Girls, invite Claudia.*
Magistrī, monēte Iūlium.	*Teachers, warn Julius.*

C. PRACTICE

Practice translating singular commands into English:

1. Studē Latīnam. _____

2. Apportā mālum. _____

3. Oppugnā lupōs. _____

Challenge: Nōn properā. _____

Now translate these plural commands.

4. Exspectāte testūdinem. _____

5. Līberī, labōrāte. _____

6. Discipulī, spectāte librōs. _____

Challenge: Puerī, nōn terrēte agnōs. _____

D. ETYMOLOGY

Commands are sometimes called *imperatives*. Study the dictionary etymology below for the word *imperative*. With the help of your teacher, write out the explanation of the etymology of *imperative*.

_____

_____

_____

Notice that the etymology sends you to a related word, *emperor*. Study the etymology of the word *emperor* and write its explanation on the lines below:

_____

_____

_____

14 Lesson Fourteen

A. FINDING THE PRESENT STEM FOR THIRD CONJUGATION VERBS

To find the present stem of third conjugation verbs, remove the *-o* ending from the **first** principal part of the verb. For example, the stem of the third conjugation verb *currō is curr-*. We can add the third conjugation present, imperfect, and future tense endings to this stem. For review, conjugate *currō* in the boxes below.

PRESENT

currō	

IMPERFECT

currēbam	

FUTURE

curram	

Now fill in the petals of the Latin flower with third conjugation endings. Use a different color for each tense. We will use *curr-* for the stem.

B. PRACTICE
Write the present stems for the third conjugation verbs below:

1. edō _____   3. scrībō _____

2. legō _____   4. carpō _____

Lesson Fourteen

C. COMMANDS FOR THIRD CONJUGATION

To make a singular command for third conjugation verbs an *-e* must be added to the present stem.

curr- (present stem) + *e* = *curre* (run - command to one person)

To make a third conjugation plural command, *-ite* must be added to the present stem.

curr + *ite* = *currite* (run - command to more than one person)

Practice forming third conjugation verbs into singular commands. The first one is done for you.

1. Eat. *Ede.* _____ 3. Write. _____

2. Read. _____ 4. Pluck. _____

Now make third conjugation plural commands. The first one is done for you.

1. Eat. *Edite.* _____ 3. Write. _____

2. Read. _____ 4. Pluck. _____

D. TRANSLATE

Translate the commands below from first, second, and third conjugations.

1. Iūlia, ede cēnam. _____

2. Puerī, apportāte prandium. _____

3. Monē coquum. _____

4. Discipulī, legite librōs. _____

5. Exspectā Claudium. _____

6. Carpe māla. _____

E. DERIVATIVE DIGGING

Look up the word *scribe* in an English dictionary and write its meaning.

scribe: _____

By adding Latin prepositions such as *in, ad,* and *sub* we can create other words. Write the meanings of these Latin prepositions on the lines. You may look them up in a Latin dictionary if necessary.

in: _____

ad: _____

sub: _____

Now look up these English derivatives formed by combining prepositions with the word *scribe*.

inscribe: _____

ascribe: _____

subscribe: _____

 # List Six

VOCABULARY

Memorize the following Latin words and their translations. Learn all four principal parts of the verbs and the genitive and gender of the nouns.

WORD	DERIVATIVE	TRANSLATION
1. mūs, mūris, *m. or f.*	_____	*mouse*
2. fēles, fēlis, *f.*	_____	*cat*
3. canis, canis, *m. or f.*	_____	*dog*
4. ungula, -ae, *f.*	_____	*claw*
5. dens, dentis, *m.*	_____	*tooth*
6. vīnum, -ī, *n.*	_____	*wine*
7. nūcleus, -ī, *m.*	_____	*kernel*
8. trīticum, -ī, *n.*	_____	*wheat*
9. marītus, -ī, *m.*	_____	*husband*
10. uxor, uxōris, *f.*	_____	*wife*
11. angulus, -ī, *m.*	_____	*corner*
12. cavum, -ī, *n.*	_____	*hole*
13. rusticus, -a, *-um*	_____	*belonging to the country, of the country*

WORD	DERIVATIVE	TRANSLATION
14. urbicus, -a, -um	_____	*belonging to the city, of the city*
15. lātrō, -āre, -āvī, -ātum	_____	*bark*
16. pōtō, -āre, -āvī, -ātum	_____	*drink*
17. occultō, -āre, -āvī, -ātum	_____	*hide*
18. insusurrō, -āre, -āvī, -ātum	_____	*whisper*
19. citō	_____	*swiftly*
20. ubī	_____	*where*

REVIEW WORDS

1. vocō, -āre, -āvī, -ātum — *call*
2. discipula, -ae, *f.* — *girl student*
3. pastor, -is, *m.* — *shepherd*
4. victor, victoris, *m.* — *winner, victor*
5. stō, -āre, stetī, -ātum — *stand*
6. testūdo, testūdinis, *f.* — *turtle, tortoise*
7. fodicō, -āre, -āvī, -ātum — *dig*
8. acūtus, -a, -um — *sharp, pointed, intelligent*

List Six

15 Lesson Fifteen

A. LINKING VERB REVIEW

Study the linking verb *sum, esse, fuī, futurum* in the present, imperfect, and future tenses. Translate the present tense.

PRESENT TENSE

sum – I am (being)	sumus –
es –	estis –
est –	sunt –

IMPERFECT TENSE

eram – I was (being)	erāmus – we were
erās – you were	erātis – you all were
erat – he, she, it was	erant – they were

FUTURE TENSE

erō – I will be	erimus – we will be
eris – you will be	eritis – you all will be
erit – he, she, it will be	erunt – they will be

N.B. Linking verbs are not followed by direct objects. Instead, they are followed by predicate nouns. Predicate nouns go in the nominative case. Study the examples below:

    Iūlia est discipul**a**.   *Julia is a (girl) student.*

Does "student" mean the same thing as Julia? Yes! Therefore, *student* is a predicate noun and must go in the nominative case. When a sentence contains a linking verb (LV) and a predicate noun (PrN), it is called a Pattern 4 sentence.

Now consider the Pattern 2 sentence below. Pattern 2 sentences contain a subject noun (SN), a verb (Vt) transitive, and a direct object (DO).

    Iūlia discipulam vocat.   *Julia calls the (girl) student.*

Does student mean the same thing as Julia? No! *Student* is a direct object.

B. FIND THE MISTAKE

The Latin sentences below contain mistakes although their English translations are correct. Try to identify the problem(s) in each sentence and write the correction on the lines provided. The first one is done as an example.

1. Iūlia est discipulam.   *Julia is a (girl) student.*

Correction: *Iūlia est discipula.*

2. Iūlia Claudia vocabat.   *Julia was calling Claudia.*

Correction: _____

3. Iūlia et Claudia sunt puellas.   *Julia and Claudia are girls.*

Correction: _____

4. Claudius et Iūlius fēles occultant.   *Claude and Julius hide the cat.*

Correction: _____

Challenge: How would you translate this sentence into Latin?

Claude and Julius hide the *cats*. _____

Lesson Fifteen

C. FORMING QUESTIONS

To form a simple question in Latin, the ending *-ne* must be added to the first word in the sentence. Usually, the first word in a Latin question is the verb. Study these examples:

Lātrat**ne** canis?	**Is** the dog barking? or **Does** the dog bark?
Lātrā**bas**ne?	**Were** you barking?
Lātrā**bit**ne fēles?	**Will** the cat bark?
Lātra**nt**ne testūdines?	**Are** the turtles barking? or **Do** the turtles bark?

Notice that the English translations of the questions begin with an appropriate helping verb. To begin a question in the present tense, choose *am/is/are* or *do/does*. In the imperfect tense, choose *was* or *were*. In the future tense, choose *will*.

Now study examples of questions using the linking verb.

Estne Iūlia discipula?	*Is Julia a (girl) student?*
Eratne Iūlius pastor?	*Was Julius a shepherd?*
Eritne Claudia coqua?	*Will Claudia be a cook?*
Sumusne amīcī?	*Are we friends?*

D. TRANSLATE

Label and translate the questions below into English. Remember to begin with correct helping verbs.

1. Pōtābitne mūs vīnum? _____

2. Stantne Iūlius et Claudius in angulō? _____

_____

3. Eratne uxor coqua? _____

4. Imperatne uxor coquam? _____

5. Fodicābatne canis cava in hortō? _____

Lesson Fifteen

E. DERIVATIVE DIGGING

Susurrant is an adjective and a derivative of *insusurrō* on List 6. Can you guess what this derivative means based on what you know about the Latin word on our list? Write your guess on the line and then look up the word *susurrant* in an English dictionary and write the meaning.

My best guess: _____

Dictionary definition: _____

16 Lesson Sixteen

A. MORE ABOUT LINKING VERBS
Label and translate the two sentences below.

Iūlius videt canem. _____

Iūlius est canis. _____

What case is used for subject nouns? _____

For direct objects? _____

For predicate nouns? _____

B. QUESTION REVIEW
Circle the correct answers about Latin questions.

1. To form a question in Latin, add the ending [*-re,   -ne,   -te*] to the first word in the sentence.

2. Usually, the first word in a Latin question is the [*subject noun,   verb,   adjective*].

3. When translating a Latin question into English, begin the question with the correct

   [*subject noun,   helping verb,   direct object*].

C. OTHER WAYS TO ASK QUESTIONS
In addition to the *-ne* ending, we can use other "question words" to form Latin questions. For example, we have already learned to use the questions *"Quid est?"* (What is it?) and *"Quis est?"* (Who is it?). Until now, we have only used *quid* and *quis* with linking verbs, but we can also use these question words to ask about what someone is doing.

Consider the examples below:

| Quis occultat? | *Who is hiding? (Who hides? Who does hide?)* |
| Quid lātrābat? | *What was barking?* |

N.B. *Quid* and *quis* are called *interrogative pronouns*.

On List 6 we have a new question word, *ubī*. *Ubī* asks the question, "Where?" and is called an *interrogative adjective*. For example:

Ubī est Iūlius?	*Where is Julius?*
Ubī sunt Iūlia et Claudia?	*Where are Julia and Claudia?*
Ubī fēles occultat?	*Where is the cat hiding?*
Ubī occultās?	*Where are you hiding?*

D. TRANSLATE
Label and translate the sentences below.

1. Habetne Iūlia fēlem? _____

2. Habetne Iūliae fēlēs ungulās? _____

3. Suntne ungulae acutae? _____

4. Ubī est fēlēs? _____

5. Vocābatne Iūlia fēlem? _____

6. Lātrābitne canis fēlem? _____

7. Fēlēsne canem terrēbat? _____

8. Ubī canis curret? _____

E. ETYMOLOGY

Choose an English derivative from List 6 and look it up in an English dictionary. Copy the etymology of your derivative on the lines below.

_____

_____

_____

What does the symbol ≤ mean? _____

List any abbreviations and tell what those abbreviations mean. For example, L = Latin.

_____

_____

_____

Lesson Sixteen

17 Lesson Seventeen

A. IN A NUTSHELL...

When people use the expression *in a nutshell*, they are summarizing information in a very short fashion. Fill in the meanings of the endings in the nutshell below.

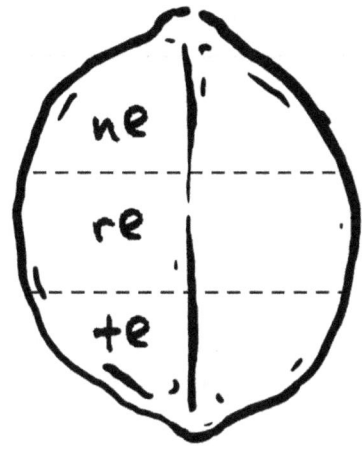

B. PREDICATE ADJECTIVES

We have learned that the linking verb is not followed by a direct object. Instead, a *predicate noun* follows the linking verb. The predicate noun renames the subject noun and is put in the nominative case. Adjectives can also follow the linking verb. Like other adjectives, they match the noun they describe in gender, number, and case, but the case will always be nominative. That is because the predicate adjective always describes the subject noun. In sentences, the predicate adjective can be labeled *PrA*.

Study the examples below.

    SN LV PrA
    Cibus est rusticus.   *The food is rustic.*

    SN   LV   PrA
    Aedificia sunt urbica.   *The buildings are urban.*

    SN   LV   PrA
    Claudia erat dēfessa.   *Claudia was tired.*

Sentences containing predicate adjectives are called Pattern 5 sentences.

C. TRANSLATE
Label and translate these Pattern 5 sentences into Latin.

1. The dog's tooth is sharp. _____

2. The cat's claws are sharp. _____

3. The wife was not foolish. _____

4. The husband is not proud. _____

5. I will be swift. _____

6. You all were tired. _____

Challenge: The wolves' teeth are sharp. _____

D. VERB PRACTICE
Translate these third conjugation verbs:

1. edit _____

2. edet _____

3. edēbat _____

4. scrībimus _____

5. scrībebāmus _____

6. scrībēmus _____

7. legō _____

8. legam _____

9. legēbam _____

Lesson Seventeen

10. carpent _____

11. carpunt _____

12. carpēbant _____

Lesson Eighteen
The Town Mouse & the Country Mouse

Translate the fable of *The Town Mouse and the Country Mouse*. You do not have to label unless you are having difficulty translating a sentence.

1. Ōlim erat* mūs rusticus. _____

2. Invītābat amīcum vīsitāre. _____

3. Amīcus est mūs urbicus et habitat in urbe. _____

4. Uxor mūris rusticī cēnam parat et amīcī edunt. _____

5. Habent glandēs, nūcleōs trīticī, et aquam. _____

6. Mūs urbicus, "Grātiae," inquit, "sed nōn est* multus cibus rurī." _____

7. Mūs urbicus mūrem rusticum invītat urbem vīsitāre. _____

8. Mūs urbicus, "Habēbimus epulās," inquit, "et edēmus cibum multum." _____

* *Erat* can sometimes be translated as "there was," and *est* can be translated as "there is."

9. Mūrēs cāseum, māla, nucēs, bācās, et mensam secundam edunt. _____

10. Pōtant vīnum. _____

11. Fēlēs et canis cito currunt ad mensam et murem rusticum terrent. _____

12. Fēlēs ungulās monstrat; canis lātrat et dentēs monstrat. _____

13. Mūs rusticus currit in cavum et occultat. _____

14. Mūs urbicus currit circum angulum mensae. _____

15. Mūs urbicus insusurrit, "Ubī ēs, mūs rusticus?" _____

16. "In cavō," rēspondet. _____

17. Mūs rusticus, "Non habeō multōs cibōs rurī," inquit, "sed nōn timeō fēlem et canem!" _____

18. Mūs rusticus currēbat ad rus ubī uxor marītum exspectābat. _____

Morum praecepta: Melior est paulum in pace quam copia in periculō.
(Better a little in peace than plenty in danger.)

FABLE GLOSSARY

1. bāca, -ae, *f.*	*berry*
2. pōmum, -ī, *n.*	*fruit*
3. epulae, -ārum, *f.*	*feast*
4. amīcus, -ī, *m.*	*friend*
5. currō, currere, cucurrī, cursum	*run*
6. devorō, -āre, -āvī, -ātum	*swallow, devour*
7. moneō, -ēre, -ui, -itum	*warn*
8. invītō, -āre, -āvī, -ātum	*invite*
9. vīsitō -āre, -āvī, -ātum	*visit*
10. mensa, -ae, *f.*	*table*
11. ūva, -ae, *f.*	*grape*
12. monstrō, -āre, -āvī, -ātum	*show*
13. terreō, -ēre, -uī, -itum	*frighten*
14. respondeō, -ēre, -dī, -sum	*answer, respond*
15. sed	*but*
16. timeō, -ēre, -uī,	*fear*
17. mūs rusticus	*country mouse*
18. mūs urbicus	*city mouse*
19. ōlim	*once upon a time*
20. parō, -āre, -avī, -ātum	*prepare*
21. gratiae	*thanks*
22. inquit	*he, she, it said*
23. glandēs	*acorns*

Lesson Eighteen

Unit Three Review

A. PRESENT TENSE VERB STEM
Fill in the blanks below.

To find the present stem of a 1st or 2nd conjugation verb, remove the ending from the

_____ principal part of the verb. To find the present stem for a 3rd conjugation verb,

remove the _____ ending from the _____ principal part of the verb.

Now give the present stems for the verbs below. They are from 1st, 2nd, and 3rd conjugations.

VERB   PRESENT STEM

1. edō, edere, ēdī, ēsum   _____

2. carpo, carpere, carpsī, carptum   _____

3. lātrō, -āre, -āvī, -ātum   _____

4. moneō, monēre, monuī, monitum   _____

B. FORMING COMMANDS
To form a singular command for 1st and 2nd conjugation verbs, simply use the present stem. Translate these English commands into Latin:

1. Hide. _____

2. Whisper. _____

3. Study. _____

Now make these same commands plural.

1. Hide. _____

2. Whisper. _____

3. Study. _____

To form a command for third conjugation verbs, re-read Lesson 14C. Now write singular commands for the verbs below.

1. Read. _____

2. Write. _____

Make the commands above plural.

1. Read. _____

2. Write. _____

C. TRANSLATE
Label and translate the Pattern 4 and Pattern 5 sentences below.

1. Mensa secunda est bona. _____

2. Fēles nōn erat canis. _____

3. Fēlēs nōn erant canēs. _____

4. Nūcleī sunt trīticum. _____

5. Dentēs canis erunt acutī. _____

6. Autumnus nōn est aestas. _____

D. QUESTION REVIEW
Fill in the blanks about questions.

To form a Latin question, add *-ne* to the _____ word in the sentence. Usually, the

first word is the _____. *Helpful Hint:* Begin your question with the correct

_____ _____.

Translate the questions below.

1. Occultābāsne? _____

2. Occultāsne? _____

3. Occultābisne? _____

4. Estne Iūlius urbicus? _____

5. Eratne Iūlia dēfessa? _____

6. Eritne Saxum dēfessum? _____

7. Quis insusurrit? _____

8. Quid est nūcleus? _____

9. Ubī occultābant Iūlia et Claudia? _____

10. Ubī est Claudius? _____

E. TRANSLATE
Label and translate the sentences below. Especially watch for third conjugation verbs.

1. Līberī multī prandium rurī edent. _____

_____

Unit Three Review

2. Saxum mensam secundam edit. _____

_____

3. Iūlia Claudiae epistulam scrībēbat. _____

_____

4. Canis murī fābulās multās leget. _____

_____

Challenge sentences:

5. Fēlēs occultant in cavō. _____

6. Fēlēs occultat in cavō. _____

F. PREPOSITION/PREFIX
The Latin preposition *ē, ex* means *out of* or *from*. List five or more English words which begin with the prefix *ex*.

_____

_____

_____

_____

_____

G. DERIVATIVES

Choose five English derivatives from Lists 5 and 6 and tell their Latin origin. Look up the definition of one of them and write it on the lines provided.

DERIVATIVE   LATIN ORIGIN

1. _____   _____

2. _____   _____

3. _____   _____

4. _____   _____

5. _____   _____

Derivative you chose: _____

Definition: _____

_____

_____

Unit Three Review

Unit 4

List Seven

VOCABULARY

Memorize the following Latin words and their translations. Learn all four principal parts of verbs and the genitive and gender of nouns.

WORD	DERIVATIVE	TRANSLATION
1. hiems, hiemis, *f.*	_____	*winter*
2. nix, nivis, *f.*	_____	*snow*
3. ventus, -ī, *m.*	_____	*wind*
4. humus, -ī, *f.*	_____	*ground, earth, soil*
5. messis, -is, *f.*	_____	*harvest*
6. hortus, -ī, *m.*	_____	*garden*
7. pānis, pānis, *m.*	_____	*bread*
8. folium, -ī, *n.*	_____	*leaf*
9. tempestās, -ātis, *f.*	_____	*weather, storm*
10. labor, labōris, *m.*	_____	*work, toil*
11. flō, -āre, -āvī, -ātum	_____	*blow*
12. legō, -ere, lēgī, lectum*	_____	*gather, collect*

* Also means *read*.

WORD	DERIVATIVE	TRANSLATION
13. niveus, -a, -um	_____	*snowy*
14. gelidus, -a, -um	_____	*cold, icy*
15. ventōsus, -a, -um	_____	*windy*
16. flāvus, -a, -um	_____	*yellow*
17. albus, -a, -um	_____	*white*
18. piger, -gra, -grum	_____	*lazy*
19. industrius, -a, -um	_____	*diligent*
20. sed (conj.)	_____	*but*

REVIEW WORDS

1. tardus, -a, -um — *slow*
2. citus, -a, -um — *swift*
3. stultus, -a, -um — *foolish*
4. superbus, -a, -um — *proud*
5. dēfessus, -a, -um — *weary*
6. malus, -a, -um — *bad*
7. niger, -gra, -grum — *black*
8. arbor, arboris, f. — *tree*

List Seven

19 Lesson Nineteen

A. VERB REVIEW

From memory, conjugate and translate *amō*, a first conjugation verb, and *dūcō*, a third conjugation verb, in the present, imperfect, and future tenses.

PRESENT TENSE

amō –	

dūcō –	

IMPERFECT TENSE

amābam –	

dūcēbam –	

FUTURE TENSE

amābō –	

dūcam –	

B. VERB SYNOPSES

A verb *synopsis* is a summary of a verb in a particular person and number. For our purposes, we will be doing verb *synopses* (the plural spelling of synopsis) in the *present, imperfect,* and *future* tenses. Study the example below. The synopsis will be done in first person singular for the verb *amō*.

TENSE	SYNOPSIS	TRANSLATION
present	amō	*I love, am loving, do love*
imperfect	amābam	*I was loving, used to love*
future	amābō	*I will love*

Now consider a synopsis for the third conjugation example *dūcō*, also in first person singular.

TENSE	SYNOPSIS	TRANSLATION
present	dūcō	*I lead, am leading, do lead*
imperfect	dūcēbam	*I was leading, used to lead*
future	dūcam	*I will lead*

C. SYNOPSIS PRACTICE
Fill in the synopses below. *Flō* is from first conjugation. *Legō* is from third conjugation.

flō in second person singular

TENSE	SYNOPSIS	TRANSLATION
present		
imperfect		
future		

legō in second person singular (Use the meaning *collect* or *gather*)

TENSE	SYNOPSIS	TRANSLATION
present		
imperfect		
future		

flō in third person singular

TENSE	SYNOPSIS	TRANSLATION
present		
imperfect		
future		

legō in third person plural (Use the meaning *collect* or *gather*)

TENSE	SYNOPSIS	TRANSLATION
present		
imperfect		
future		

D. DERIVATIVE DIGGING

Write a descriptive paragraph or a very short story using at least ten derivatives from List 7. <u>Underline</u> the derivatives you use.

20 Lesson Twenty

A. ADJECTIVE REVIEW

An adjective describes a noun or a pronoun. It can tell what kind, which one, or how many. Adjectives must match the nouns they describe in *gender, number,* and *case*. Fill in the blanks below about noun-adjective agreement.

1. What are the three genders? List the chant ending which goes with each gender.

GENDER   **ENDING**

_____   _____

_____   _____

_____   _____

2. What is meant by number?

_____

_____

3. What are the five noun cases? List the parts of speech that go with each noun case.

CASE	PART OF SPEECH
_____	_____
_____	_____
_____	_____
_____	_____
_____	_____

B. PRACTICE
Circle the correct translations for the noun-adjective phrases below.

1. lazy Julius (nominative)   a. Iūlius pigra   b. Iūlius piger   c. Iūlius pigrum

2. lazy Julia (dative)   a. Iūliae pigrae   b. Iūliae pigris   c. Iulia pigro

3. yellow leaves (nominative)   a. folia flāvī   b. folia flāvae   c. folia flāva

4. white snow (accusative)   a. nivem albam   b. nivem album   c. nivem albem

5. the snowy tree (nominative)   a. arbor niveum   b. arbor niveae   c. arbor nivea

6. windy weather (nominative)   a. tempestas ventosī   b. tempestas ventosās   c. tempestas ventosa

Piger is one of many adjectives that end in *-er* in the masculine singular in the nominative case. As with all adjectives, the base of the adjective is found by removing the feminine ending. In a word such as *piger, pigra, pigrum*, this results in a spelling change. What is the base for this adjective?

_____

Lesson Twenty

C. FORMING ADVERBS

To form an adverb in Latin, remove the ending from the feminine form and add *-e*. Frequently, the English adverb will add the ending -ly. Study the examples below and then create adverbs from the remaining adjectives.

FEM. ADJ.	BASE	ADVERB	TRANSLATION
1. gelida	gelid	gelide	coldly
2. pigra			
3. industria			
4. stulta			
5. superba			

D. TRANSLATION

Translate these sentences into Latin.

1. Does the cold wind blow coldly? _____

2. Diligent Julia gathers the harvest diligently. _____

_____

3. The lazy dog barks lazily. _____

E. ETYMOLOGY

Look up the word *humble* in an English dictionary and write its etymology on the lines below.

_____

_____

Lesson Twenty

List Eight

VOCABULARY

Memorize the following Latin words and their translations. Learn all four principal parts of verbs and the genitive and gender of nouns.

WORD	DERIVATIVE	TRANSLATION
1. formīca, -ae, *f.*	_____	*ant*
2. gryllus, -ī, *m.*	_____	*grasshopper*
3. fidēs, -ium, *f.*	_____	*lute, lyre, harp*
4. colōnia, -ae, *f.*	_____	*colony*
5. rēgīna, -ae, *f.*	_____	*queen*
6. sapientia, -ae, *f.*	_____	*wisdom*
7. mīca, -ae, *f.*	_____	*crumb*
8. fames, famis, *f.*	_____	*hunger, starvation*
9. parō, -āre, -āvī, -ātum	_____	*prepare*
10. laudō, -āre, -āvī, -ātum	_____	*praise*
11. errō, -āre, -āvī, -ātum	_____	*wander, err*
12. saltō, -āre, -āvī, -ātum	_____	*dance*
13. reservō, -āre, -āvī, -ātum	_____	*save, lay up, reserve*

WORD	DERIVATIVE	TRANSLATION
14. amō, -āre, -āvī, -ātum	_____	*like, love*
15. augeō, -ēre, auxī, auctum	_____	*increase*
16. celēbrō, -āre, -āvī, -ātum	_____	*celebrate*
17. canō, -ere, cecinī, cantum	_____	*play (on an instrument)*
18. per (prep. w/acc.)	_____	*through*
19. trans (prep. w/acc.)	_____	*across*
20. diu (adv)	_____	*for a long time*

REVIEW WORDS

1. do, -āre, dedī, -ātum   *give*
2. cavum, -ī, *n.*   *hole*
3. rogo, -āre, -āvī, -ātum   *ask*
4. cibus, -ī, *m.*   *food*
5. edo, -ere, ēdī, ēsum   *eat*
6. nūcleus, -ī, *m.*   *kernel*
7. trīticum, -ī, *n.*   *wheat*
8. portō, -āre, -āvī, -ātum   *carry*
9. stultus, -a, -um   *foolish*
10. sub (prep w/ abl.)   *under*
11. aestas, aestātis, *f.*   *summer*
12. autumnus, -ī, *m.*   *autumn*
13. habitō, -āre, -āvī, -ātum   *live in, inhabit*
14. cīvis, -is, *m.* or *f.*   *citizen*
15. parens, parentis, *m.* or *f.*   *parent*
16. praedium, -ī, *n.*   *farm*
17. timeō, -ēre, timuī, ——   *fear*
18. quod   *because*

21 Lesson Twenty-One

A. SYNOPSIS REVIEW

Do a synopsis of the verb *augeō* in the first person plural.

TENSE	SYNOPSIS	TRANSLATION
present		
imperfect		
future		

Now do a synopsis of the verb *edō* in the second person plural.

TENSE	SYNOPSIS	TRANSLATION
present		
imperfect		
future		

B. PRACTICE DECLENSIONS

Fill in the missing parts of the noun declension charts below from memory. Then use your charts to check your answers. Correct any spelling errors.

FIRST DECLENSION

-a	
	-īs
-am	

SECOND DECLENSION

-us	-ī
-ō	

SECOND DECLENSION NEUTER

-um	
	-ōrum
-ō	

THIRD DECLENSION

-x	
-is	
	-ibus

C. THIRD DECLENSION I-STEM NOUNS

Below is a variation of the third declension. It is called an *i-stem* because of the extra *-i* in the genitive plural. Highlight the genitive plural ending.

THIRD DECLENSION I-STEM

NOM.	-is	-ēs
GEN.	-is	-ium
DAT.	-ī	-ibus
ACC.	-em	-ēs
ABL.	-e	-ibus

Here are two rules for identifying masculine and feminine third declension i-stem nouns (a third rule for neuter nouns will be introduced later.)

RULE #1: If a noun ends in *-is* or *-es* in the nominative singular, and the nominative and genitive singular have the same number of syllables, then the noun is an i-stem.

Here are some i-stems which obey this rule.

Nom.	famēs	auris	fēles
Gen.	famis	auris	felis

N.B. The word *canis* is an exception to this rule.

RULE #2: If a noun ends in *-s* or *-x* in the nominative singular, and its base ends in two consonants, then the noun is an i-stem.

Underline the base of the nouns below. (N.B. *Don't try to change the case until you find the base. The genitive case is the place to find the base!*)

Nom.	dens	mons
Gen.	dentis	montis

For the i-stem nouns below, tell whether they obey Rule #1 or Rule #2 by writing a *1* or *2* on the blanks. Then write the meanings. You may look up words in the glossary if you don't remember. These nouns are taken from word lists we have studied in the past.

THIRD I-STEM NOUN	RULE	TRANSLATION
1. ovis, ovis	_____	_____
2. urbs, urbis	_____	_____
3. parens, parentis	_____	_____
4. nox, noctis	_____	_____
5. cīvis, cīvis	_____	_____

D. TRANSLATE
Label and translate the sentences below.

1. Erat hiems et līberī et Saxum nivem gelidam spectābant. _____

2. Ventus gelidus flābat per arborēs. _____

3. Saxum Iūliō et Iūliae colōniam formīcārum sub humō monstrābat. _____

4. Formīcae labōrābant aestāte* et cibum legēbant in hortō. _____

5. Formīcae nōn erant pigrae. _____

* *Aestāte* means "in the summer." It does not require a preposition in Latin.

Lesson Twenty-One

E. DERIVATIVE DIGGING

Look up the English derivative *auction* and write its definition on the lines.

auction: _____

_____

Which word from List 8 is the Latin origin of *auction*? _____

22 Lesson Twenty-Two

A. I-STEM REVIEW
Fill in the blanks for the third declension i-stem rules below.

RULE #1: If a noun ends in _____ or _____ in the nominative singular, and the nominative and genitive singular have the same number of _____, then the noun is an i-stem.

RULE #2: If a noun ends in _____ or _____ in the nominative singular, and its base ends in two _____, then the noun is an i-stem.

B. I-STEM IDENTIFICATION
Below are third declension nouns we have learned in the past. Even if you don't remember what the words mean you should be able to identify whether or not they are i-stems by using the rules above. If the word is an i-stem write *yes*. If not, write *no*.

THIRD DECL. NOUN	I-STEM?
1. carcer, carceris	_____
2. avis, avis	_____
3. frutex, fruticis	_____
4. iūdex, iūdicis	_____
5. infans, infantis	_____
6. vulpēs, vulpis	_____

C. TRANSLATE
Label and translate the sentences below into Latin. Remember to think carefully about endings!

1. Julia has a farm of ants. _____

2. Julia's ants dig holes in the garden. _____

3. The ants prepare the queen a colony. _____

4. The ants gather crumbs of food in summer.* _____

_____

5. In the winter* the ants will dance and play the lute. _____

_____

6. Do the ants fear the snow? _____

Challenge: The ants do not fear the snow because they have food. _____

_____

N.B. The preposition *of* indicates what noun case? _____

D. ETYMOLOGY
Look up the word *sapient* and write its etymology on the lines below.

_____

_____

_____

_____

* *Aestate* means "in the summer." *Hieme* means "in the winter." These phrases do not need a preposition in Latin.

23 Lesson Twenty-Three

A. VERB SYNOPSES PRACTICE

Do a synopsis of the third conjugation verb *legō* in first person singular.

TENSE	SYNOPSIS	TRANSLATION
present		
imperfect		
future		

Do a synopsis of the first conjugation verb *errō* in the second person plural.

TENSE	SYNOPSIS	TRANSLATION
present		
imperfect		
future		

B. TRANSLATE ADVERBS

Translate these sentences containing adverbs:

1. Formīcae labōrābant industrie. _____

2. Ventus flat gelide. _____

3. Gryllus errābit pigre. _____

4. Hortus auget tarde. _____

C. MACARONIC STORY
Write a short macaronic story using at least ten Latin words from Lists 7 and 8. <u>Underline</u> the Latin words.

_____
_____
_____
_____
_____
_____
_____
_____
_____
_____

Challenge
Label and translate the following sentence into Latin:
Cold Julia will prepare cold Rock's cold snow for cold Julius on the cold ground coldly!

_____
_____
_____
_____

Lesson Twenty-Three

Lesson Twenty-Four
The Grasshopper & the Ants

Translate the fable *The Grasshopper and the Ants*. You do not have to label unless you are having difficulty translating a sentence.

1. Erat aestās et formīcae industriae diū labōrābant in hortō. _____

2. Legēbant mīcās et nūcleōs trīticī edere hieme.* _____

3. Gryllus stultus cantābat et fidibus canābat aestāte.** _____

4. Rēgīna formīcārum formīcās industrias laudābat quod formīcae sapientiam multam habēbant. ___

5. Gryllus sapientiam nōn habēbat. _____

6. Gryllus rīdēbat et formīcās dēfessās spectābat sed formīcae mīcās et nūcleōs reservābant. _____

* *Hieme* is the ablative of *hiems* and can mean *in the winter*.
** *Aestate* is the ablative of *aestas* and means *in the summer*.

7. Messis formīcārum augēbat. _____

8. Nunc est hiems et formīcae habitant sub humō niveā in colōniā. _____

9. Rēgīna formīcīs cibum bonum dant et formīcae cantant et saltant et celēbrant! _____

10. Tempestās est gelida et ventus flat. _____

11. Gryllus gelidus tarde ambulat ad colōniam formīcārum. _____

12. "Dā mihi*** cibum," inquit, "quod famem habeō." _____

13. "Ubī erās," rēgīna inquit, "aestāte?" _____

14. "Labōrābāsne?" rēgīna rogat. _____

*** *Dā mihi* means "give (to) me."

Lesson Twenty-Four

15. "Nōn amō," gryllus inquit, "labōrāre aestāte." _____

_____

16. "Igitur," rēgīna inquit, "nōn potes saltāre hieme." _____

_____

Morum praecepta: Qui nōn labōrat nōn edit. *(He who does not work does not eat).*

FABLE GLOSSARY

1. cantō, -āre, -āvī, -ātum — *sing*
2. edō, edere, ēdī, ēsum — *eat*
3. multus, -a, -um — *much, many*
4. rīdeō, -ēre, rīsī, risum — *laugh*
5. nunc — *now*
6. dēfessus, -a, -um — *tired*
7. sub (prep w/abl.) — *under*
8. igitur — *then*
9. inquit — *he, she, it said*
10. quod — *because*
11. ubī — *where*
12. tardus, -a, -um — *slow*
13. citus, -a, -um — *swift, fast*
14. habeō, -ēre, habuī, habitum — *have*
15. possum, posse, potuī, —— — *be able*

Lesson Twenty-Four

Unit Four Review

A. VERB SYNOPSIS

Fill in the verb synopses below. Pay attention to the person and number for each synopsis.

1. Second person, singular, for the first conjugation verb *saltō*

TENSE	SYNOPSIS	TRANSLATION
present		
imperfect		
future		

2. First person, plural, for the second conjugation verb *augeō*

TENSE	SYNOPSIS	TRANSLATION
present		
imperfect		
future		

3. Third person, singular, for the third conjugation verb *legō* (when it means "gather, collect")

TENSE	SYNOPSIS	TRANSLATION
present		
imperfect		
future		

B. NOUN-ADJECTIVE AGREEMENT

Answer the questions about noun-adjective agreement.

1. What are the three genders? Which declension goes with each gender?

   GENDER

   _____

   _____

   _____

   DECLENSION

   _____

   _____

   _____

2. What is meant by number?

   _____

   _____

3. What are the five noun cases and what part of speech does each case represent?

   CASE

   _____

   _____

   _____

   _____

   _____

   PART OF SPEECH

   _____

   _____

   _____

   _____

   _____

C. ADVERBS
Answer the following questions about adverbs and then translate the adverbs listed.

1. Which gender of the adjective is used to find the base? _____

2. How do you form an adverb from an adjective? _____

Translate adverbs:

1. gelide _____

2. industrie _____

3. lazily _____

D. THIRD DECLENSION CHANTS
Fill in the third declension and third declension i-stem chants from memory and then check your work. Spelling counts.

THIRD DECLENSION

-x	

THIRD DECLENSION I-STEM

-is	

E. I-STEM RULES
Fill in the blanks for both of the third declension i-stem rules below and give an example of each.

RULE #1: If a noun ends in -*is* or -*es* in the _____ _____,

and the nominative and _____ singular have the _____

number of syllables, then the noun is an i-stem.

Example: _____

RULE #2: If a noun ends in -s or -x in the _____ _____,

and its base ends in _____ _____, then the noun is an i-stem.

Example: _____

F. TRANSLATE
Label and translate the sentences below.

1. Diū formīcae industriae cibum augent aestāte. _____

2. Rēgīna labōrem industrium formīcārum laudābat. _____

3. Iūlius et Iūlia messem in hortō legent. _____

4. Gryllus piger nōn saltat in humō niveā. _____

Unit Four Review

5. The grasshopper has hunger because he does not lay up food. _____

_____

6. The diligent ants will prepare the queen a colony. _____

_____

G. DERIVATIVES

List ten derivatives and their Latin origins from Lists 7 and 8.

DERIVATIVE	LATIN ORIGIN
1. _____	_____
2. _____	_____
3. _____	_____
4. _____	_____
5. _____	_____
6. _____	_____
7. _____	_____
8. _____	_____
9. _____	_____
10. _____	_____

Unit 5

 # List Nine

VOCABULARY

Memorize the following Latin words and their translations. Learn the principal parts of verbs and the genitive and gender of nouns.

WORD	DERIVATIVE	TRANSLATION
1. leō, leōnis, *m.*		*lion*
2. iuba, -ae, *f.*		*mane of any animal*
3. pēs, pedis, *m.*		*foot, paw*
4. misericordia, -ae, *f.*		*pity, mercy*
5. vēnātor, -ōris, *m.*		*hunter*
6. plaga, -ae, *f.*		*net (for hunting)*
7. fūnis, fūnis, *m.*		*rope*
8. humī		*on the ground*
9. implōrō, -āre, -āvī, -ātum		*beg, implore (w/tears)*
10. līberō, -āre, -āvī, -ātum		*free, set free*
11. iaceō, -ēre, -uī		*lie*
12. ligō, -āre, -āvī, -ātum		*bind*
13. iactō, -āre, -āvī, -ātum		*throw*

WORD	DERIVATIVE	TRANSLATION
14. fremō, -ere, -uī, -itum	_____	*roar, growl*
15. trahō, -ere, traxī, tractum	_____	*drag*
16. fugitō, -āre, -āvī, -ātum	_____	*flee (from)*
17. administrō, -āre, -āvī, -ātum	_____	*help, manage*
18. rōdō, -ere, rōsī, rōsum	_____	*nibble, gnaw*
19. ferus, -a, -um	_____	*fierce*
20. super (prep. w/acc.)	_____	*over, above*

REVIEW WORDS

1. mūs, mūris, *m.* — *mouse*
2. dens, dentis, *m.* — *tooth*
3. somnus, -ī, *m.* — *sleep*
4. possum, posse, potuī, —— — *be able*
5. iuvō, -āre, iūvī, iūtum — *help*
6. obsecrō, -āre, -āvī, -ātum — *beg, implore*
7. īrātus, -a, -um — *angry*
8. parvus, -a, -um — *little, small*
9. acūtus, -a, -um — *sharp, pointed (also intelligent)*
10. māgnus, -a, -um — *large*
11. ē, ex (prep. w/abl.)* — *out of, from*

* Use with the prepositional phrase *ē somnō*.

List Nine

DEMONSTRATIVE PRONOUN: HIC, HAEC, HOC

Review and be able to spell the chant below. It means *this, these*. Remember to memorize these two charts *across*, not down.

SINGULAR: THIS

Masculine	Feminine	Neuter
hic →	haec	hoc
huius →	huius	huius
huic →	huic	huic
hunc →	hanc	hoc
hōc →	hāc	hōc

PLURAL: THESE

Masculine	Feminine	Neuter
hī →	hae	haec
hōrum →	hārum	hōrum
hīs →	hīs	hīs
hōs →	hās	haec
hīs →	hīs	hīs

List Nine

25 Lesson Twenty-Five

A. CONJUGATE LINKING VERBS
Conjugate and translate the linking verb in the present, imperfect, and future tenses.

PRESENT TENSE

sum –	

IMPERFECT TENSE

eram –	

FUTURE TENSE

erō –	

B. REVIEW PERSONAL PRONOUNS

From memory, fill in the personal pronoun chants below. When you finish, use your chant charts to correct any misspellings. You do not have to give the missing meanings. Your teacher will help you do that.

PERSONAL PRONOUNS (FIRST PERSON)

SINGULAR

ego – I

PLURAL

nōs – we

PERSONAL PRONOUNS (SECOND PERSON)

SINGULAR

tū – you

PLURAL

vōs – you all

C. SHOWING EMPHASIS

Compare the following sentence pairs.

First Person:	Sum leō.	*I am a lion.*
	Ego sum leō.	*I am a lion.*
Second Person:	Es vēnātor.	*You are a hunter.*
	Tū es vēnātor.	***You*** *are a hunter.*

Notice that both pairs of sentences mean the same thing in English. *Sum leō* and *ego sum leō* both mean "I am a lion." The difference comes in emphasis, a difference we are more likely to hear when the

sentence is spoken. In writing, we rely on bold letters or some other trick to show where the emphasis lies. The first sentence, "*Sum leō,*" is merely a statement of fact. In the second version, "*Ego sum leō,*" we emphasize that *I* am the lion and no one else!

In the sentence "*Es vēnātor,*" we are again stating a fact. But when we add the pronoun *tū*, as in "*Tū es vēnātor,*" we are emphazing that *you* are the hunter (and not the lion). The Romans often omitted separate pronouns and instead relied on verb endings to tell who the subject pronoun was. When they wanted to give special attention to the pronoun, they would use some form of *ego* or *tū*. Now study the plural examples below.

First Person:	Sumus lēonēs.	*We are lions.*
	Nōs sumus leōnēs.	***We** are lions.*
Second Person:	Estis vēnātōrēs.	*You all are hunters.*
	Vōs estis vēnātōrēs.	***You all** are hunters.*
Third Person	Sunt bovēs	*They are cows.*
	Iī/eae/ea sunt	***They** are cows.*

D. TRANSLATE

Label and translate these Pattern 4 sentences into English. Subject pronouns can be labeled as SP. Highlight any pronouns requiring special emphasis in both the Latin and English versions. The first two are done as examples.

```
   LV  PrN
1. Sum mūs.            I am a mouse.

   SP    LV    PrN
2. Nōs  sumus  līberī.   We are children.
```

3. Tū es parvus. _____

4. Es parvus. _____

5. Estis pastōrēs. _____

6. Vōs estis cursōrēs. _____

7. Ego sum testūdō. _____

8. Tū nōn es testūdo. _____

9. Estis tardī. _____

10. Nōs nōn sumus puellae. _____

E. DERIVATIVE DIGGING

Look up the English derivative *rodent* and read the definitions. Then list several animals (in English) that are rodents.

_____

_____

_____

26 Lesson Twenty-Six

A. DEMONSTRATIVE PRONOUNS AS ADJECTIVES

Study the demonstrative chant *hic* that follows List 9 and be able to spell it correctly. Then fill in the missing parts of the chant from memory. When you finish, correct your work.

SINGULAR

Masculine	Feminine	Neuter
hic		
	huius	
		huic
hunc		
	hāc	

PLURAL

Masculine	Feminine	Neuter
		haec
hōrum		
	hīs	
hōs		
		hīs

Lesson Twenty-Six 163

You already know that the demonstrative above means *this, these*. Demonstratives can be used as pronouns or adjectives. In this lesson, we will use them as adjectives. Like any other adjective, they must match the noun they describe in gender, number, and case.

Study the feminine examples below and label the parts of speech in both the English and Latin examples.

This girl throws Claudia the rope.	*Haec puella* Claudiae fūnem iactat.
Claudia throws *this girl* the rope.	Claudia *huic puellae* fūnem iactat.
Claudia helps *this girl*.	Claudia *hanc puellam* administrat.
These girls throw Claudia.	*Hae puellae* Claudiam iactant.

Now consider some masculine examples and label them.

This lion flees (from) the hunter.	*Hic leō* vēnātōrem fugitat.
The hunter flees (from) *this lion*.	Vēnātor *hunc leōnem* fugitat.
The hunter shows *this lion* mercy.	Vēnātor *huic leōnī* misericordiam monstrat.
The mice gnaw *this lion's* rope.	Mūrēs fūnem *huius leōnis* rodunt.

B. TRANSLATE

Label and translate the sentences below.

1. Līberī et Saxum leōnēs spectābant in Rōmā. _____

_____

2. Leō prīmus fremebat et līberōs terrēbat. _____

_____

3. Vēnātor hanc plāgam super hunc leōnem iactat. _____

_____

4. Hic vēnātor fūnem habet et pedēs huius leōnis ligat. _____

_____

5. Hic leō iacet humī et vēnātor leōnem trahit. _____

6. Hī leōnēs vēnātōrem implōrant hunc leōnem līberāre. _____

C. PERSONAL PRONOUN REVIEW
Label and translate the sentences below. When a personal pronoun is used, highlight it in both Latin and English.

1. Ego hunc vēnātōrem administrābō sed tū leōnem ligābis. _____

2. Tū huic vēnātōrī hunc fūnem iactās. _____

3. We will flee (from) these lions. _____

4. You all are growling. _____

D. ETYMOLOGY
Look up the word *adjacent* and write its etymology on the lines below.

Lesson Twenty-Six

Now write a definition of *adjacent*.

_____

_____

_____

Lesson Twenty-Six

List Ten

A. VOCABULARY

Memorize the following Latin words and their translations. Learn the principal parts of verbs and the genitive and gender for nouns.

WORD	DERIVATIVE	TRANSLATION
1. beneficium, -ī, *n.*	_____	*kindness*
2. vestīgium, -ī, *n.*	_____	*footprint, track*
3. silva, -ae, *f.*	_____	*forest*
4. vīta, -ae, *f.*	_____	*life*
5. pellis, -is, *f.*	_____	*hide, skin*
6. animal, -is, *n.*	_____	*animal*
7. mare, -is, *n.*	_____	*sea*
8. caput, capitis, *n.*	_____	*head*
9. corpus, corporis, *n.*	_____	*body*
10. iūrō, -āre, -āvī, -ātum	_____	*swear, take an oath*
11. capiō, -ere, cēpī, captum*	_____	*capture*
12. reddō, -ere, -didī, -ditum	_____	*repay*

* This word is actually a third conjugation i-stem verb.

WORD	DERIVATIVE	TRANSLATION
13. dērīdeō, -ēre, -rīsī, -rīsum	_____	*mock*
14. vestīgō, -āre, -āvī, -ātum	_____	*track (verb)*
15. dubitō, -āre, -āvī, -ātum	_____	*doubt, hesitate*
16. grātus, -a, -um	_____	*pleasing, grateful*
17. maestus, -a, -um	_____	*sad*
18. sī placet	_____	*please*
19. dum	_____	*while*
20. ā, ab (prep. w/abl.)	_____	*from, away from*

REVIEW WORDS

1. rīdeō, -ēre, rīsī, rīsum — *laugh, smile*
2. ungula, -ae, *f.* — *claw*
3. monstrō, -āre, -āvī, -ātum — *show, point out*
4. apportō, -āre, -āvī, -ātum — *bring*
5. do, -āre, dedī, dātum — *give*
6. clamō, -āre, -āvī, -ātum — *shout*
7. sub (prep. w/acc.) — *under*
8. rēx, rēgis, *m.* — *king*

brevī somnō ūtor — *I take a nap*	brevī somnō ūtimur — *we take a nap*
brevī somnō ūteris — *you take a nap*	brevī somnō ūtimini — *you all take a nap*
brevī somnō ūtitur — *he, she, it takes a nap*	brevī somnō ūtuntur — *they take a nap*

27 Lesson Twenty-Seven

A. DEMONSTRATIVE PRONOUN REVIEW

Practice writing the demonstrative chant *hic, haec, hoc*. Use a different color for each gender.

SINGULAR

Case	Masculine	Feminine	Neuter
Nom.	hic	haec	hoc
Gen.			
Dat.			
Acc.			
Abl.			

PLURAL

Case	Masculine	Feminine	Neuter
Nom.			
Gen.			
Dat.			
Acc.			
Abl.			

Give the singular meaning of this chant. _____

What is the plural meaning? _____

When a demonstrative is used as an adjective, it must match the noun it describes in what three ways?

_____, _____, _____

Do adjectives (demonstrative or otherwise) always match the noun they describe in *declension*? _____

B. TRANSLATE

Now translate the phrases below into Latin according to the case given. You also need to think about the gender and number of each word. The first is done as an example.

1. this lion (acc.) _____*hunc leōnem*_____

2. these forests (nom.) _____

3. this king (dat.) _____

4. this footprint (nom.) _____

5. this net (abl.) _____

6. these paws (gen.) _____

C. THIRD DECLENSION NEUTER

We have learned the regular third declension noun endings. Now we will meet another third declension "cousin," the third declension neuter. Compare the chants below and highlight the endings in third declension neuter which are different.

THIRD DECLENSION

-x	-ēs
-is	-um
-ī	-ibus
-em	-ēs
-e	-ibus

THIRD DECLENSION NEUTER

-x	-a
-is	-um
-ī	-ibus
-x	-a
-e	-ibus

N.B. Like second declension neuter nouns, third neuter nouns also look the same in the nominative and accusative cases. Circle the nominative and accusative endings for third declension neuter in the chant on the previous page.

Now circle the correct demonstrative adjective form for the noun-adjective phrases below. Only the nominative case will be used. Be sure to pay attention to gender and number.

1. this body: *hic*   *haec*   *hoc*   corpus

2. these heads: *hī*   *hae*   *haec*   capita

D. TRANSLATE
Label and translate the sentences below. The last one needs to be translated from English into Latin.

1. Iūlius Claudiō vestīgia māgna in hāc silvā monstrat. _____

2. Sunt vestīgia huius leōnis. _____

3. Iūlius et Claudius hunc leōnem vestīgant dum Saxum hōs fūnēs apportat. _____

4. Puerī hanc plāgam super leōnem iactant et Saxum pēdēs leōnis ligat. _____

5. Puerī clamant, "Nōs sumus vēnātōrēs!" _____

6. Iūlia et Claudia sunt sub pelle leōnis! _____

7. These girls laugh and mock the boys. _____

Lesson Twenty-Seven

E. ETYMOLOGY

When we hear the term *capital*, we usually think of a city that is a seat of government such as a state capital or a nation's capital. But a capital can also be used in architecture. The Romans used many pillars topped by capitals in their buildings. Here is the dictionary etymology for *capital*:

[ME.< Ofr. *chapitel*<L. *capitellum*, dim. of *caput*, the HEAD].

Tell why this etymology makes sense.

_____

_____

28 Lesson Twenty-Eight

A. THIRD DECLENSION NEUTER I-STEM

The third declension has many cousins! We have met three members of the third declension noun family so far: third declension, third declension i-stem, and third declension neuter. The last member of this family is the *third declension neuter i-stem*. Compare it with the third declension neuter. Highlight the places where the i-stem is different.

THIRD DECLENSION NEUTER

-x	-a
-is	-um
-ī	-ibus
-x	-a
-e	-ibus

THIRD DECLENSION NEUTER I-STEM

-x	-ia
-is	-ium
-ī	-ibus
-x	-ia
-ī	-ibus

We have learned two rules for recognizing third declension nouns when they are masculine or feminine. Now we will learn a third rule for recognizing third declension neuter i-stems.

Rule #3: If the noun is neuter, and the nominative singular ends in *-al* or *-e*, the noun is an i-stem.

Two very common nouns which obey this rule are *animal* and *mare*. *Animal* is declined for you. Decline *mare* in the same way. Highlight the endings on both paradigms (declined words).

N.B. Remember . . . *Don't try to change the case until you find the base. The genitive case is the place to find the base!*

animal	animālia
animālis	animālium
animālī	animālibus
animāl	animālia
animālī	animālibus

mare	
maris	

B. PRACTICE
Circle the form of the demonstrative adjective *hic, haec, hoc* which matches the noun in gender and number. You will be told which case to use. The first one is done as an example. You may use your book or charts.

NOMINATIVE CASE | | | | **LATIN NOUN**
1. this forest: | hic | (haec) | hoc | silva
2. this king: | hic | haec | hoc | rēx
3. these footprints: | hī | hae | haec | vestīgia

GENITIVE CASE | | | | **LATIN NOUN**
1. of this animal: | huius | hōrum | hoc | animālis
2. of this life: | huic | hanc | huius | vītae
3. of these nets: | hīs | hārum | hī | plagārum

DATIVE CASE | | | | **LATIN NOUN**
1. to, for this hunter: | hunc | huic | hāc | vēnātōrī
2. to, for these girls: | hīs | hae | hanc | puellīs
3. to, for this body: | haec | hōc | huic | corporī

ACCUSATIVE CASE | | | | **LATIN NOUN**
1. this head: | hunc | hanc | hoc | caput
2. this hide, skin: | hunc | hanc | hoc | pellem
3. this lion: | hunc | hanc | hoc | leōnem

C. TRANSLATE
Label and translate these Pattern 4 sentences. Highlight the personal pronouns in your translation.

1. Ego sum hic vēnātor. _____

2. Tū es hic rex hōrum animālium. _____

3. Nōs sumus hī puerī. _____

4. Vōs estis hae puellae. _____

Lesson Twenty-Eight

Challenge: Translate this sentence into Latin. Keep in mind whether you are a boy or a girl, and be sure to use a personal pronoun.

I am this student. _____

D. PREPOSITIONS

Use an English dictionary to look up five words beginning with the prefix *super*. Choose one of these words and write the definition.

1. _____

2. _____

3. _____

4. _____

5. _____

Word you are defining: _____

Definition: _____

_____

Lesson Twenty-Eight

29 Lesson Twenty-Nine

A. CHANT CHECK
Fill in the personal pronoun chants below from memory. Check your work and make corrections in red. You do not have to give meanings.

PERSONAL PRONOUNS (FIRST PERSON)

SINGULAR

ego – I

PLURAL

nōs – we

PERSONAL PRONOUNS (SECOND PERSON)

SINGULAR

tū – you

PLURAL

vōs – you all

B. TRANSLATE

Translate the Pattern 4 & Pattern 5 sentences below containing linking verbs into Latin. When personal pronouns are italicized for emphasis in English be sure to use the Latin personal pronouns in your translation. The first two are done as examples.

1. I am a lion. *Sum leō.*

2. *I* am a lion. *Ego sum leō.*

3. You were a hunter. _____

4. *We* will be kings. _____

5. You all are not fierce. _____

6. I am a mouse but *you all* are lions. _____

_____

C. ANOTHER CHANT CHECK

Fill in the demonstrative chant below from memory. When you are finished, look up the chant and check your work. Correct any errors in red.

SINGULAR

Masculine	Feminine	Neuter
hic		

Lesson Twenty-Nine

PLURAL

Masculine	Feminine	Neuter
hī		

D. CHALLENGE

Label and translate the challenge sentence below. Remember to make the demonstrative adjectives match the nouns they describe in gender, number, and case.

Challenge: This hunter tracks this lion's footprints away from this forest. _____

_____

_____

30 Lesson Thirty
The Lion & the Mouse

Translate the fable *The Mouse and the Lion*. You do not have to label unless you are having difficulty translating a sentence.

1. Ōlim leō humī iacēbat sub arbōre et brevī somnō ūtebatur.* _____

_____

2. Mūs trans corpus leōnis et per iubam currēbat dum leō brevī somnō ūtebatur. _____

_____

_____

3. Hic mūs parvus hunc leōnem māgnum excitābat. _____

_____

4. Leō fremēbat et pedēs māgnōs in mūrem pōnēbat. _____

_____

5. Mūs maestus leōnem implōrābat, "Habē misericordiam!" _____

_____

6. "Sī placet, mē** līberā." _____

* *Ūtebatur* is in the imperfect tense. See Review Words on List Ten.
** *Me* is the accusative of *ego* and means me.

7. Mūs, "Iurō tē*** administrāre," inquit, "et reddam beneficium." _____

8. Leō rīdēbat et mūrem dērīdēbat. _____

9. Leō, "Tū," inquit, "nōn potes mē administrāre." _____

10. "Tū es parvus mūs et ego sum māgnus leō!" _____

11. Sed leō mūrī misericordiam monstrābat et mūrem līberābat. _____

12. Vēnātōrēs animālia vestīgābant et leōnem inlaqueābant. _____

13. Vēnātōrēs hanc plāgam super leōnem iactābant et pedēs leōnis ligābant. _____

14. Leō fremēbat dum vēnātōrēs leōnem trahēbant ē silvā. _____

15. Hīc mūs et amīcī currēbant leōnem et administrant. _____

*** *Te* is the accusative of *tu* and means you.

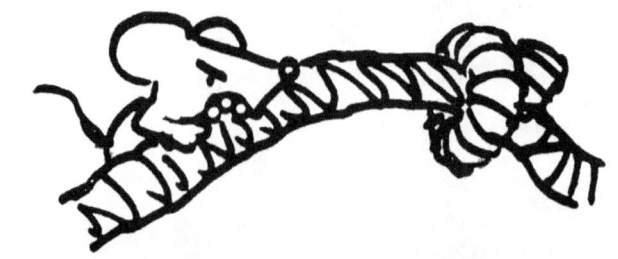

16. Hī mūrēs fūnēs rodēbant et leōnem grātum līberābant. _____

_____

17. Leō mūrēs laudābat! _____

Morum praecepta: Una benevolentia meret alia *(One good turn deserves another)*.

FABLE GLOSSARY

ōlim (adv.)	*once upon a time*
arbor, arbōris, *f.*	*tree*
trans (prep w/ acc.)	*across, over*
per (prep w/ acc.)	*through*
currō, currere, cucurrī, cursum	*run*
excitō, -āre, -āvī, -ātum	*wake*
pōnō, pōnere, posuī, positum	*put, place*
habeo, -ēre, habuī, habitum	*have*
inlaqueō, -āre, -āvī, -ātum	*entrap, ensnare*
amīcus, -ī, *m.*	*friend*
implōrō, -āre, -āvī, -ātum	*beg*

Lesson Thirty

Unit Five Review

A. FOUR PRINCIPAL PARTS: VERB REVIEW

Write out the missing principal parts and meanings of these second and third conjugation verbs from memory. Then look them up and correct your spelling in red.

1ST PART	2ND PART	3RD PART	4TH PART	MEANING
fremō				
trahō				
reddō				
dērīdeō				
iaceō				

B. GENITIVES & GENDERS: NOUN REVIEW

Give the genitive, gender, and translation for the following third declension nouns.

WORD	GENITIVE	GENDER	TRANSLATION

1. leō	_____	_____	_____

2. corpus	_____	_____	_____

3. fūnis	_____	_____	_____

4. mare	_____	_____	_____

5. rēx	_____	_____	_____

6. pellis	_____	_____	_____

WORD	GENITIVE	GENDER	TRANSLATION
7. animal	_____	_____	_____
8. caput	_____	_____	_____
9. vēnātor	_____	_____	_____
10. pes	_____	_____	_____

C. THIRD DECLENSION I-STEM RULES

Study the three rules for identifying third declension i-stem nouns and then write the correct rule on the blank next to the noun. If the word is not a third i-stem, write "NOT!"

RULE #1: If a noun ends in *-is* or *-es* in the nominative singular, and the nominative and genitive singular have the same number of syllables, then the noun is an i-stem.

RULE #2: If a noun ends in *-s* or *-x* in the nominative singular, and its base ends in two consonants, then the noun is an i-stem.
N.B. Rules #1 and #2 apply to masculine and feminine nouns only.

RULE #3: If the noun is neuter, and the nominative singular ends in *-al* or *-e*, the noun is an i-stem.

THIRD I-STEM NOUN   **RULE #**

1. pellis, pellis, *f.* _____

2. corpus, corporis, *n.* _____

3. animal, animālis, *n.* _____

4. fūnis, fūnis, *m.* _____

5. rēx, rēgis, *m.* _____

6. dens, dentis, *m.* _____

7. mare, maris, *n.* _____

D. TRANSLATE

Translate these Pattern 4 sentences containing forms of the linking verb, relative pronouns, and the demonstrative adjective. Be sure to label first.

1. Hae puellae erant grātae. _____

2. Ego sum vēnātor sed tū es leō. _____

3. Nōs erimus rēgēs. _____

4. This hide is small. _____

5. This animal was fierce. _____

6. These bodies were animals. _____

E. DEMONSTRATIVE ADJECTIVE PRACTICE

Fill in the blanks with the correct form of the demonstrative adjective *hic, haec, hoc*. Then label and translate the sentences. The demonstrative adjective should agree with the noun that *follows* it.

1. _____ rēx iurābit./ _____

2. Reddēs Iūliō _____ beneficium./ _____
   _____

3. Vēnātōrēs _____ plāgās trahent./ _____
   _____

4. Saxum _____ animal liberat./ _____
   _____

5. Mūs _____ fūnes rodēbant./ _____

F. DERIVATIVE STORY
Write a short story using at least ten derivatives from lists 9 and 10. <u>Underline</u> the derivatives you use.

Unit 6

 # List Eleven

VOCABULARY

Memorize the following Latin words and their translations. Learn the principal parts of the verbs and the genitive and gender for nouns.

WORD	DERIVATIVE	TRANSLATION
1. grāculus, -ī, *m.*		*jackdaw*
2. pinna, -ae, *f.*		*feather*
3. avis, avis, *f.*		*bird*
4. pāvō, pāvōnis, *m.*		*peacock*
5. columba, -ae, *f.*		*pigeon, dove*
6. aquila, -ae, *f.*		*eagle*
7. anas, anatis, *f.*		*duck*
8. rīvus, -ī, *m.*		*stream*
9. Iuppiter, Iovis, *m.*		*Jupiter*
10. vellō, -ere, vellī, vulsum		*pluck*
11. adfīgō, -ere, fīxī, fīxum*		*fasten to, affix*

* *Adfigo* is used with the preposition *ad*. For example: *Puella globulum ad pallam adfigit.* The girl is fastening a button to her cloak

WORD	DERIVATIVE	TRANSLATION
12. convocō, -āre, -āvī, -ātum	_____	*call together*
13. dēligō, -ere, -lēgī, -lectum	_____	*select, choose*
14. gestō, -āre, -āvī, -ātum	_____	*wear*
15. lavō, -āre, lāvī, lautum	_____	*wash*
16. foedus, -a, -um	_____	*ugly*
17. pulcher, -chra, -chrum	_____	*beautiful, handsome*
18. vānus, -a, -um	_____	*vain*
19. māgnificus, -a, -um	_____	*magnificent*
20. inter (prep. w/acc.)	_____	*between, among*

REVIEW WORDS

1. legō, -ere, lēgī, lectum — *gather*
2. carpō, -ere, carpsī, carptum — *pluck (as in fruit)*
3. globulus, ī, *m.* — *button*
4. vestis, vestis, *f.* — *clothing*
5. coma, -ae, *f.* — *hair, leaves*

DEMONSTRATIVE PRONOUN: ILLE, ILLA, ILLUD

Memorize the new chant below. It is also a demonstrative pronoun or adjective chant and means *that, those*.

SINGULAR: THAT

Masculine	Feminine	Neuter
ille	illa	illud
illīus	illīus	illīus
illī	illī	illī
illum	illam	illud
illō	illā	illō

PLURAL: THOSE

Masculine	Feminine	Neuter
illī	illae	illa
illōrum	illārum	illōrum
illīs	illīs	illīs
illōs	illās	illa
illīs	illīs	illīs

31 Lesson Thirty-One

A. VERB TENSE REVIEW

From memory, fill in the present, imperfect, and future tense verb endings and meanings for first and second conjugation verbs.

PRESENT TENSE

-ō –	

IMPERFECT TENSE

-bam –	

FUTURE TENSE

-bō –	

Fill in the present, imperfect, and future tense verb endings and meanings for third conjugation verbs. Remember, third conjugation endings look different from first and second.

PRESENT TENSE

-ō —	

IMPERFECT TENSE

-ēbam —	

FUTURE TENSE

-am —	

B. PERFECT TENSE

Now we will be introduced to the *perfect tense*. The perfect tense is the *other* past tense (we have already learned the imperfect tense). The good news is that the perfect tense uses the same set of endings whether the verb is from first, second, or third conjugations!

Study the perfect tense paradigm (chart) below. We will use the helping verbs *has/have* but note the other possible ways to translate the perfect tense.

PERFECT TENSE

Helping verbs: *-ed (not really a helping verb but an ending), has/have, did*

-ī – *I have*	-imus – *we have*
-istī – *you have*	-istis – *you all have*
-it – *he, she, it has*	-ērunt – *they have*

The perfect tense does not use the *present stem* as do the present, imperfect, and future. Instead, we must attach the perfect endings to what is called the *perfect stem*.

Before learning how to find the perfect stem, we should review how to find the present stem:

First and Second Conjugation

To find the present stem of a 1st or 2nd conjugation verb, remove the _____ ending from the

_____ principal part of the verb.

Third Conjugation

To find the present stem of a 3rd conjugation verb, remove the _____ ending from the

_____ principal part.

The perfect stem is found by removing the *-ī* ending from the third principal part of the verb. This is true for all three conjugations we have learned. Consider our new Latin flower which we can call the *perfect stem flower*. We will use the first conjugation verb *amō, amāre, amāvī, amātum* as our example.

What is the perfect stem for *amō, amāre, amāvī, amātum*? _____

Lesson Thirty-One

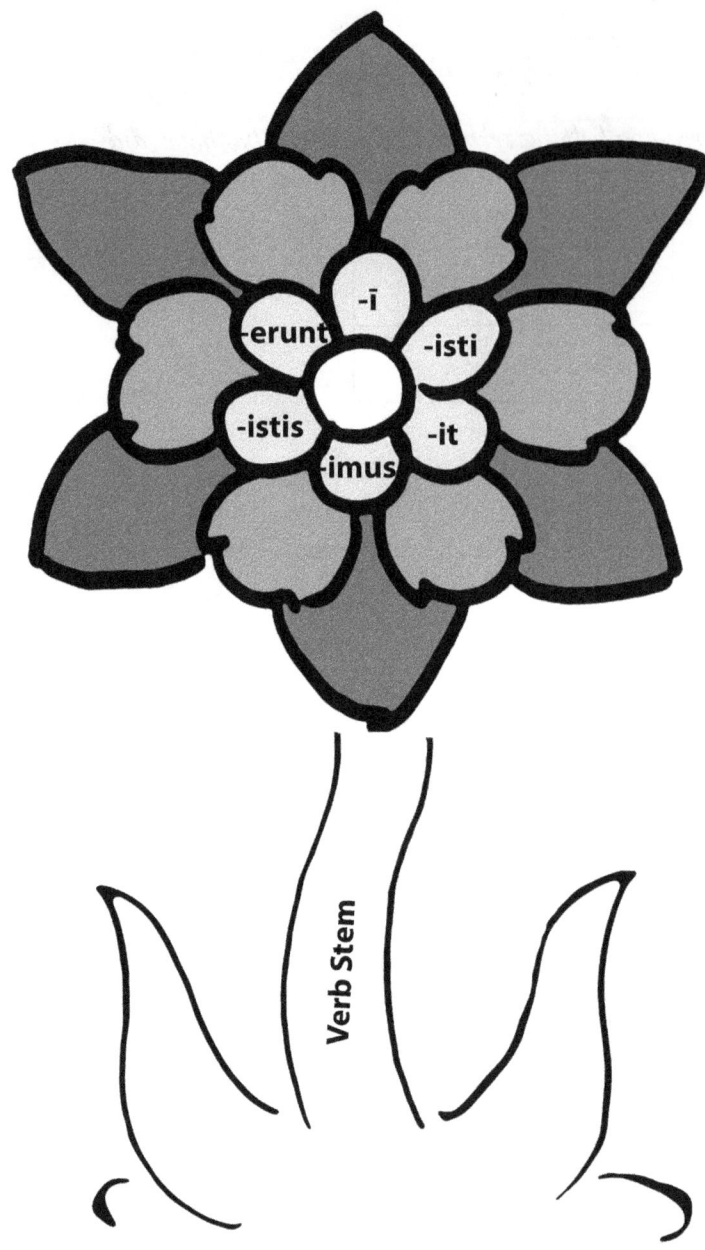

Using the third principal part, find the perfect stem for *adfigō, adfigere, adfixī, adfixum*. Then fill in the perfect stem and perfect endings for this verb on the following flower.

N.B. We will be adding two more layers of petals to the "perfect" flower in future lessons.

C. FIND THE STEMS

Practice finding the present and perfect stems for the verbs below. One is done as example. Pay attention to the conjugation of each verb.

VERB	PRESENT STEM	PERFECT STEM
1. lavō, -āre, lāvī, lautum	lava-	lav-
2. dēligō, -ere, dēlēgī, dēlēctum	_____	_____

Lesson Thirty-One

VERB	PRESENT STEM	PERFECT STEM

3. vellō, -ere, vellī, vulsum _____ _____

4. gestō, -āre, -āvī, -ātum _____ _____

5. adfīgō, -ere, adfīxī, adfīxum _____ _____

D. TRANSLATE
Practice translating these verbs in the perfect tense.

1. adfīxit _____

2. vellimus _____

3. convocāvērunt _____

4. gestāvistī _____

5. lavī _____

6. dēlēgistis _____

E. PREPOSITION PRACTICE
The Latin preposition *inter* is used as a prefix on many English words. With the help of an English dictionary, write at least ten derivatives that begin with *inter-*. Then look up one of them and write its definition on the lines provided.

Derivatives with *inter-*: _____

_____

Your word: _____

Definition: _____

_____

200 Lesson Thirty-One

32 Lesson Thirty-Two

A. PRACTICE WITH PERFECT TENSE
Practice translating these perfect tense verbs into Latin.

1. We have washed _____

2. You all did call together _____

3. I selected _____

4. You did wear _____

5. They plucked _____

6. She has fastened _____

B. MORE PRACTICE
Circle the correct translation for the verbs below. Be sure to identify the conjugation and tense of each verb!

1. adfīgit	*he did affix*	*she affixes*	*they will affix*
2. dēlīget	*he was selecting*	*he will select*	*he does select*
3. gestābunt	*they will wear*	*we will wear*	*they were wearing*
4. lāvērunt	*we have washed*	*they will wash*	*they did wash*
5. convocābam	*we called together*	*I called together*	*I was calling together*

Challenge: Circle the correct Latin translation.

you all plucked   *vellitis*   *vellistis*   *velletis*

C. TRANSLATE
Label and translate the sentences below. All verbs are in the perfect tense.

1. Līberī avēs vestīgāvērunt in silvā. _____

2. Iūlia vestīgia columbae spectāvit et līberōs convocāvit. _____

3. Claudius et Saxum pinnās vidērunt humī. _____

4. Līberī et Saxum hās pinnās lāvērunt et pinnās adfīxērunt ad vestem. _____

5. Claudia pinnam pāvōnis in comā gestāvit. _____

6. Iūlius pinnās anatis in rīvō legit. _____

7. Līberī et Saxum pinnās pulchrās legērunt. _____

Lesson Thirty-Two

D. CHANT CHECK
Fill in the missing parts of the demonstrative chant *ille, illa, illud*.

SINGULAR: THAT

Masculine	Feminine	Neuter
ille	illa	illud
	illam	
		illō

PLURAL: THOSE

Masculine	Feminine	Neuter
illī		illa
		illōrum
illōs		
		īllīs

E. ETYMOLOGY
Look up the derivative *pen* (the kind you write with) in a dictionary and write its etymology on the lines below.

pen: _____

_____

_____

_____

 # List Twelve

A. VOCABULARY

Memorize the following Latin words and their translations. Learn the principal parts of the verbs and the genitive and gender of nouns.

WORD	DERIVATIVE	TRANSLATION
1. caelum, -ī, *n.*	_____	*sky, heaven(s)*
2. rīpa, -ae, *f.*	_____	*bank (of river, stream)*
3. mundus, -ī, *m.*	_____	*world*
4. nīdus, -ī, *m.*	_____	*nest*
5. caeruleus, -a, -um	_____	*blue*
6. viridis, -e*	_____	*green*
7. ruber, rubra, rubrum	_____	*red*
8. aureus, -a, -um	_____	*golden*
9. niger, -gra, -grum	_____	*black*
10. explōrō, -āre, -āvī, -ātum	_____	*explore*
11. cantō, -āre, -āvī, -ātum	_____	*sing*
12. intellegō, -ere, -lēxī, -lēctum	_____	*realize, understand*

* *Viridis, -e* is a third declension adjective.

WORD	DERIVATIVE	TRANSLATION
13. dēflō, -āre, -āvī, -ātum		*blow away*
14. imperō, -āre, -āvī, -ātum		*order*
15. accūsō, -āre, -āvī, -ātum		*accuse*
16. nūntiō, -āre, -āvī, -ātum		*announce*
17. cumulō, -āre, -āvī, -ātum		*heap, pile up*
18. prope (prep. w/acc.)		*near*
19. quoque		*also*
20. tum		*then*

REVIEW WORDS

1. flāvus, -a, -um — *yellow*
2. auscultō, -āre, -āvī, -ātum — *listen to*
3. turgeō, -ēre, tursī, ____ — *swell up*
4. volō, -āre, -āvī, -ātum — *fly*
5. quod — *because*
6. superbus, -a, -um — *proud*
7. multus, -a, -um — *much, many*
8. culpō, -āre, -āvī, -ātum — *blame*
9. humus, -ī, *f.* — *ground, earth, land*
10. terra, -ae, *f.* — *ground, earth, land*
11. spectō, -āre, -āvī, -ātum — *look at, watch*
12. terreō, -ēre, -uī, -itum — *frighten*
13. videō, -ēre, vīdī, vīsum — *see*
14. sedeō, -ēre, sēdī, sessum — *sit*
15. ōvum, -ī, *n.* — *egg*
16. ubī — *where*
17. -ne — *question ending*

List Twelve

33 Lesson Thirty-Three

A. LEARNING TO TELL THE DIFFERENCE
One of the confusing aspects of third conjugation verbs is the similarity between the present and perfect tense endings. Circle the places on the chants below where the present and perfect look the same.

PRESENT TENSE: 3ʳᵈ CONJUGATION

-ō	-imus
-is	-itis
-it	-unt

PERFECT TENSE: 3ʳᵈ CONJUGATION

-ī	-imus
-istī	-istis
-it	-ērunt

When the endings look the same, how do you tell which tense is being used? The answer lies in which verb stem is being used.

Study the third conjugation verb below and underline the present and perfect verb stems.

intellego   *intellegere*   *intellēxī*   *intellēctum*

Now compare the tranlsations of various forms of this verb. Underline or highlight the stem on each verb.

PRESENT	intellegit	*he, she, it realizes, (is realizing, does realize)*
PERFECT	intellēxit	*he, she, it realized, (has realized, did realize)*
PRESENT	intellegimus	*we realize, (are realizing, do realize)*
PERFECT	intellēximus	*we realized, (have realized, did realize)*
PRESENT	intellegitis	*you all realize, (are realizing, do realize)*
PERFECT	intellēxistis	*you all realized, (have realized, did realize)*

B. TRANSLATE

Here are some other third conjugation verbs to translate. Be sure to consult your third conjugation charts and pay close attention to verb stems and endings. All four tenses we have studied (present, imperfect, future, and perfect) may be used. Underline verb stems and circle verb endings.

1. intellegent _____

2. intellegunt _____

3. intellēxērunt _____

4. adfīxit _____

5. adfigit _____

6. adfiget _____

7. adfigēbat _____

8. dēligis _____

9. dēligēs _____

10. dēlēgistī _____

Challenge: The present and perfect verb stems for *vello, vellere, vellī, vulsum* look the same. Both are *vell-*. In that case, how do you tell whether or not the verb below is present or perfect?

    vellit   *he plucks*
    vellit   *he plucked*

In a situation like this you must rely on context clues in the sentence or paragraph. Translate the sentences below.

Hodiē Iūlius pinnās vellit. _____

Herī Iūlius pinnās vellit. _____

Lesson Thirty-Three

C. MORE TRANSLATION

Use your chant chart to help you translate phrases using the *ille, illa, illud* (meaning *that/those*). All are in the nominative case.

1. ille mundus   *that world*

2. illud caelum _____

3. illī nīdī _____

4. illa rīpa _____

5. illa caela _____

6. illae columbae _____

Now supply the correct form of *ille* to go with the accusative nouns below.

1. *illam* _____ columbam

2. _____ rīvōs

3. _____ grāculum

4. _____ pinnās

5. _____ caelum

6. _____ vestīgia

Challenge: Translate the phrase *"those ducks"* in the nominative case.

_____

D. DERIVATIVE DIGGING

Look up the derivative *aquiline* in an English dictionary and write the definition on the lines below. Then tell its Latin origin.

aquiline: _____

_____

Latin origin: _____

34 Lesson Thirty-Four

A. MORE PRACTICE WITH VERB SYNOPSES

Fill in the verb synopses below. All are in third person singular. You may use your chant charts.

cantō in third person singular (first conjugation) / *cantō, cantāre, cantāvī, cantātum*

TENSE	SYNOPSIS	TRANSLATION
present		
imperfect		
future		
perfect		

videō in third person singular (second conjugation) / *videō, vidēre, vīdī, vīsum*

TENSE	SYNOPSIS	TRANSLATION
present		
imperfect		
future		
perfect		

intellegō in third person singular (third conjugation) / *intellegō, intellegere, intellēxī, intellēctum*

TENSE	SYNOPSIS	TRANSLATION
present		
imperfect		
future		
perfect		

B. TRANSLATE

Label and translate the sentences below which contain the demonstrative adjectives *hic* and *ille* and the perfect tense.

1. Līberī et Saxum anatēs spectāvērunt prope rīvum. _____

2. Claudia hanc rīpam explōrāvit sed Iūlia explōrāvit illam rīpam. _____

3. Illī puerī ambulāvērunt in hāc rīpā et hās anatēs terruērunt. _____

4. Claudia quoque illās anatēs terruit. _____

5. Tum illae anatēs volāvērunt ā hōc rīvō ad illam terram. _____

6. Saxum in hāc rīpā nīdum vīdit. _____

7. In illō nīdō ōva anatis erant.* _____

8. Māter Anas sēdit in illīs ōvīs.** _____

Erant = there were   ** *Ōvis* is the ablative plural of *ōvum*. It does not mean "sheep."

C. ANSWER THE QUESTIONS

Answer the following Latin questions about section B of this lesson. You may answer in English but use complete sentences for your answers. (Challenge: Try to answer the questions in Latin.)

1. Ubī līberī et Saxum anatēs spectāvērunt? _____

Challenge answer: _____

2. Explōrāvēruntne Claudia et Iūlia rīpās? _____

Challenge answer: _____

3. Quis anatēs terruit? _____

Challenge answer: _____

4. Ubī anatēs volāvērunt? _____

Challenge answer: _____
_____

5. Quid est in nīdō? _____

Challenge answer: _____
_____

D. DERIVATIVE DIGGING

Choose one of the following derivatives and correctly use it in a sentence. You may need to look up your derivative in an English dictionary first.

Derivative choices: *celestial, riparian, deflate, imperative, enunciate*

Sentence: _____
_____

Lesson Thirty-Four

35 Lesson Thirty-Five

A. TRANSLATE
Translate the groups of verbs below into Latin. Pay attention to whether the verb is from first, second, or third conjugation.

1. we will realize _____

2. we do realize _____

3. we did realize _____

4. they are fastening (to) _____

5. they did fasten (to) _____

6. they will fasten (to) _____

7. I am singing _____

8. I have sung _____

9. I will sing _____

10. you will see _____

11. you see _____

12. you saw _____

13. she chooses _____

14. she chose _____

15. she will choose _____

B. DEMONSTRATIVE ADJECTIVE PRACTICE

On each blank, write the correct demonstrative adjective (*hic, haec, hoc* . . . or *ille, illa, illud* . . .) to agree with the noun it describes in gender, number, and case. Then translate the sentence. The first one is done as an example.

1. Iūlia (*this*) __hanc__ pinnam rubram vellit.

    Julia plucks (or plucked) this red feather.

2. (*That*) _____ columba est alba.

    _____

3. Līberī (*these*) _____ avēs vident sed (*those*) _____ avēs nōn vident.

    _____

    _____

4. Iūlius (*this*) _____ avī (*that*) _____ nīdum monstrat.

    _____

Challenge: Ubī est (*that*) _____ rīvus?

    _____

C. IDENTIFY

Use a colored pencil or marker to show the color of each Latin word below.

1. viridis, -e
2. ruber, -bra, -brum
3. caeruleus, -a, -um
4. aureus, -a, -um
5. niger, -gra, -grum

Lesson Thirty-Five

36 Lesson Thirty-Six
The Vain Jackdaw

Translate the fable of *The Vain Jackdaw*. You do not have to label unless you are having difficulty translating a sentence.

1. Iuppiter avēs convocāvit prope rīvum. _____

2. "Crās," nūntiāvit, "ego dēligam rēgem avium." _____

3. "Dēligam," inquit, "avem pulcherrimam." _____

4. Erant multae avēs pulchrae. _____

5. Anas caput viride habuit. _____

6. Aquila erat magna et superba. _____

7. Columba erat quoque pulchra et pinnās albās habuit. _____

8. Sed pulcherrima avis erat pāvo. _____

9. Pāvō longās pinnās magnificās gestāvit. _____

10. Huius pāvōnis pinnae erant viridēs, caeruleae, et aureae. _____

11. Grāculus vānus nōn erat pulcher sed erat foedus. _____

12. Pinnae grāculī erant nigrae. _____

13. Furtim hic grāculus pinnās hārum avium vellit dum lāvērunt in rīvō. _____

14. Grāculus hās pinnās cumulāvit prope hunc rīvum. _____

15. Grāculus pinnās adfīxit ad suum corpus. _____

16. Iuppiter avēs spectāvit. _____

17. "Grāculus," inquit, "est pulcherrima avis." _____

18. "Hic grāculus," Iuppiter nūntiavit, "erit rēx avium." _____

19. Sed pāvō pinnam vellit ā grāculō. _____

20. Anas, columba, et aquila pinnās quoque vellērunt ā hōc grāculō. _____

21. Iuppiter vēritātem intellēxit. _____

22. "Tū es," Iuppiter inquit, "grāculus vānus." _____

_____

23. "Dēligam pāvōnem esse rēgem." _____

_____

Morum praecepta: Pinnae pulchrae nōn faciunt aves pulchrae *(Fine feathers do not make fine birds)*

FABLE GLOSSARY

1. crās — *tomorrow*
2. pulcherrimus, -a, -um — *most beautiful*
3. erant — *there were*
4. habuit — *had (perfect tense)*
5. furtim — *secretly*
6. dum — *while*
7. esse — *to be (infinitive of sum)*
8. suus, sua, suum — *his, her, its*

Lesson Thirty-Six

Unit Six Review

A. PRESENT & PERFECT TENSE REVIEW
Fill in the blanks about finding present and perfect tense verb stems and helping verbs.

1. To find the *present stem* for first and second conjugation verbs, go to the _____ principal part of the verb and remove the ending _____ .

2. To find the *present stem* of third conjugation verbs, go to the _____ principal part of the verb and remove the ending _____ .

3. The five helping verbs for the present tense are: _____, _____, _____, _____, _____ .

4. To find the *perfect stem* for first, second, and third conjugation verbs, go to the _____ principal part of the verb and remove the ending _____ .

5. Helping verbs for the perfect tense are _____, _____/_____ , _____ .

B. CHANT CHECK

From memory, fill in the missing parts of the demonstrative pronoun/adjective chant *ille*:

SINGULAR: THAT

Masculine	Feminine	Neuter
ille		
	illius	
		illī
illum		
	illā	

PLURAL: THOSE

Masculine	Feminine	Neuter
		illa
illōrum		
	illīs	
		illa
illīs		

C. FIRST, SECOND, & THIRD CONJUGATION REVIEW

Fill in the verb endings and meanings below. First and second conjugations use the same endings while third conjugation has its own endings.

FIRST & SECOND CONJUGATIONS

Present Tense

-ō –	

Imperfect Tense

-bam –	

Future Tense

-bō –	

THIRD CONJUGATION

Present Tense

-ō –	

Imperfect Tense

-ēbam –	

Future Tense

-am –	

D. PERFECT TENSE

Fill in the perfect tense endings and meanings. The perfect tense uses the same endings in first, second, and third conjugations.

Perfect Tense

-i –	

Unit Six Review

E. CONJUGATION IDENTIFICATION

Give the conjugation and the present and perfect stems of the verbs below. The first one is done as an example.

VERB	CONJ.	PRESENT STEM	PERFECT STEM
1. dēligō	3rd	dēlig-	dēleg-
2. gestō	_____	_____	_____
3. adfīgō	_____	_____	_____
4. terreō	_____	_____	_____

F. VERB PRACTICE

Translate the verbs below. Label the tense of each. Pay attention to the verb stem. The first two are done as examples.

VERB	TENSE	TRANSLATION
1. intellegit	present	he, she, it realizes (is realizing, does realize)
2. intellēxit	perfect	he, she, it realized (has realized, did realize)
3. accūsābāmus	_____	_____
4. accūsāvimus	_____	_____
5. vellis	_____	_____
6. vellistī	_____	_____
7. dēligam	_____	_____
8. gestābō	_____	_____
9. adfīxistis	_____	_____
10. adfīgitis	_____	_____

Challenge:

1. dēligimus _____ _____

2. dēlēgimus _____ _____

3. dēligemus _____ _____

G. SYNOPSIS

Do a verb synopsis for *adfigo* in the second person singular:

TENSE	SYNOPSIS	TRANSLATION
present		
imperfect		
future		
perfect		

H. SENTENCE PRACTICE

Label and translate these sentences.

1. Iuppiter illum grāculum vānum accūsāvit. _____

_____

2. Ille grāculus erat foedus sed hic pāvō est pulcher. _____

_____

3. Illae avēs pinnās caeruleās et rubrās gestāvērunt. _____

_____

4. Iūlius et Iūlia illam anatem prope hunc rivum dēligunt. _____

_____

5. Claudius Claudiam nōn intellegit. _____

6. Hodiē nōs adfīgimus pinnās ad canem, sed herī vōs adfīxistis pinnās ad fēlem. _____

_____

I. DERIVATIVES
Write a derivative to go with each of the Latin words below:

WORD   DERIVATIVE

1. dēflō _____

2. imperō _____

3. aquila _____

4. dēligō _____

5. vānus _____

6. caelum _____

7. intellegō _____

8. avis _____

Unit 7

List Thirteen

VOCABULARY

Memorize the following Latin words and their translations. Learn the principal parts of the verbs and the genitive and gender of nouns.

WORD	DERIVATIVE	TRANSLATION
1. lāc, lactis, *n.*	_____	*milk*
2. lactaria, -ae, *f.*	_____	*dairy maid*
3. mulctra, -ae, *f.*	_____	*milk pail*
4. cella, -ae, *f.*	_____	*storeroom*
5. cella lactaria	_____	*dairy*
6. vacca, -ae, *f.*	_____	*cow*
7. gallīna, -ae, *f.*	_____	*hen*
8. pullus, -ī, *m.*	_____	*chicken or chick*
9. ōvum, -ī, *n.*	_____	*egg*
10. gradus, -ūs, *m.**	_____	*braid*
11. macellum, -ī, *n.*	_____	*market*
12. novus, -a, -um	_____	*new*

* *Gradus, -us* is from the fourth declension.

WORD	DERIVATIVE	TRANSLATION
13. possum, posse, potui, ——	_____	*be able, can*
14. pariō, -ere, peperī, partum**	_____	*bear, bring forth*
15. ōva parere	_____	*to lay eggs*
16. emō, -ere, ēmī, emptum	_____	*buy*
17. vēnditō, -āre, āvī, -ātum	_____	*sell*
18. dormītō, -āre, -āvī, -ātum	_____	*dream*
19. exclūdō, -ere, -clūsī, -clūsum	_____	*shut out, exclude* (for birds: *hatch*)
20. ante (prep. w/acc.)	_____	*before*

REVIEW WORDS

1. legō, -ere, lēgī, lēctum — *gather, collect*
2. caput, capitis, *n.* — *head*
3. augeō, -ēre, auxī, auctum — *increase*
4. deflō, -āre, -āvī, -ātum — *blow away*
5. deridēō, -ēre, -risi, risum — *mock*
6. administrō, -āre, -āvī, -ātum — *help, manage*
7. iaceō, -ēre, -ui, ---- — *lie*
8. cumulō, -āre, -āvī, -ātum — *heap, pile up*
9. trahō, -ere, traxī, tractum — *drag*
10. fremō, -ere, -uī, -itum — *roar, growl*
11. nīdus, -ī, *m.* — *nest*
12. labōrō. -āre, -āvī -ātum — *work*
13. curō, -āre, -āvī, -ātum — *care for*
14. praedium, -ī, *n.* — *farm*
15. do, -āre, dedi, datum — *give*
16. habeō, -ere, -uī, -itum — *have*
17. ancilla, ae, *f.* — *maid*
18. horreum, -ī, *n.* — *barn*

** *Pario* is a third conjugation i-stem verb. In some of its forms, you will notice an extra *i*.

List Thirteen

37 Lesson Thirty-Seven

A. VERB TENSE REVIEW
Translate the first and second conjugation verbs below from the present, imperfect, future, and perfect tenses.

1. vēnditābō _____

2. dormītābant _____

3. dērīdēs _____

4. dērīsistī _____

5. cumulāvērunt _____

6. iacēbimus _____

7. iacuimus _____

8. iacēmus _____

9. administrābam _____

10. dēflāvit _____

11. dēflābit _____

12. augent _____

B. TRANSLATE
Translate these third conjugation verbs from the present, imperfect, future, and perfect tenses.

1. exclūdit _____

2. exclūsit _____

3. pariō _____

4. peperī _____

5. trahimus _____

6. trahēmus _____

7. traximus _____

8. fremēbātis _____

9. fremitis _____

10. fremuistis _____

Challenge:

1. emunt _____

2. ēmērunt _____

3. ement _____

C. PLUPERFECT TENSE

We have learned that the perfect stem is found by removing the ending from the _____ principal part of the verb. We have also learned that the perfect tense endings *-ī, -istī, -it, -imus, -istis, -ērunt* can be attached to the perfect stem. Now we will learn another tense that also attaches to the perfect stem. It is called the *pluperfect tense.*

Study the pluperfect endings and their meanings below:

PLUPERFECT TENSE ENDINGS

-eram – *I had*	-erāmus – *we had*
-erās – *you had*	-erātis – *you all had*
-erat – *he, she, it had*	-erant – *they had*

In the space below draw a Latin flower. Label the stem as "The Perfect Stem." Draw a layer of six petals and write the perfect tense endings on the petals. Then draw another layer of six petals and write the pluperfect endings on them.

D. TRANSLATE
Underline endings and translate these verbs in the pluperfect tense. The first one is done as an example.

1. ēmerāmus — *we had bought*

2. pepererant — _____

3. vēnditāverat — _____

4. dormītāverātis — _____

5. exclūserās — _____

6. intellēxeram — _____

E. ETYMOLOGY
Write the etymology for the derivative *poultry*.

Poultry: _____

N.B. *Pullet* shares the same etymology with *poultry*. What is a pullet? If you don't know, look it up in a dictionary.

Pullet: _____

38 Lesson Thirty-Eight

A. TRANSLATE

Label and translate the sentences below. Underline verb endings and circle any verbs in the pluperfect tense.

1. Iūlia labōrābat in praediō et pullōs cūrābat. _____

2. Agricola Iūliae gallīnam dederat. _____

3. Gallīna Iūliae ōva pepererat et sedēbat in nīdō. _____

4. Claudia Iūliam vīsitābat et iuvābat ōva legere in horreō. _____

5. Sed puellae nōn lēgerant ōva gallīnae Iūliae quod gallīna Iūliae pullōs parvōs in ōvīs* habuit!

_____

_____

*Ablative plural of *ōvum*.

B. VERB SYNOPSIS PRACTICE
Complete the verb synopses below. Be sure to use the correct verb stems.

vēnditō in second person singular (first conjugation)

TENSE	SYNOPSIS	TRANSLATION
present	vēnditās	you sell
imperfect		
future		
perfect		
pluperfect		

emō in second person singular (third conjugation)

TENSE	SYNOPSIS	TRANSLATION
present	emis	you buy
imperfect		
future		
perfect		
pluperfect		

C. TRANSLATING VERBS

Translate these verbs into Latin. Pay attention to helping verbs. Give the tense for each.

	TRANSLATION	TENSE
1. she bears	_____	_____
2. she bore	_____	_____
3. she had born	_____	_____
4. we were dreaming	_____	_____
5. we will dream	_____	_____
6. we had dreamed	_____	_____
7. they had hatched	_____	_____
8. they will hatch	_____	_____
9. they have hatched	_____	_____

D. DERIVATIVE DIGGING

Choose one derivative from list 13 and look it up in a dictionary. Write the definition and Latin origin on the lines provided.

Derivative: _____

Latin Origin: _____

Definition: _____

_____

Lesson Thirty-Eight

14 List Fourteen

VOCABULARY

Memorize the following Latin words and their translations. Learn the principal parts of the verbs and the genitive and gender of nouns.

WORD	DERIVATIVE	TRANSLATION
1. agricola, -ae, *m.*	_____	*farmer*
2. adulēscēns, adulēscentis, *m.*	_____	*young man*
3. virgō, virginis, *f.*	_____	*young woman, maiden*
4. oculus, -ī, *m.*	_____	*eye*
5. gena, -ae, *f.**	_____	*cheek**
6. stola, -ae, *f.*	_____	*dress*
7. calceus, -ī, *m.*	_____	*shoe, slipper*
8. pecūnia, -ae, *f.*	_____	*money*
9. convīvium, -ī, *n.*	_____	*party*
10. saltātiō, -ōnis, *f.*	_____	*a dance*
11. bellus, -a, -um	_____	*pretty*
12. roseus, -a, -um	_____	*rosy, pink*

* *Gena* usually appears in the plural (*genae*).

List Fourteen 239

WORD	DERIVATIVE	TRANSLATION
13. ēvānēscō, ēvānēscere, ēvānuī, ——	_____	*vanish, disappear*
14. numerō, -āre, -āvī, -ātum	_____	*count*
15. mulgeō, mulgēre, mulsī, ——	_____	*milk*
16. quatiō, quatere, quassī, quassum	_____	*shake*
17. effundō, -ere, -fūdī, -fūsum	_____	*spill, pour out*
18. cadō, -ere, cecidī, casum	_____	*fall*
19. mereō, -ēre, -uī, -itum	_____	*earn, deserve*
20. dē (prep. w/abl.)	_____	*down from, about, concerning*

REVIEW WORDS

1. flāvus, -a, -um — *yellow, blond*
2. caeruleus, -a, -um — *blue*
3. caput, capitis, *n.* — *head*
4. fīlia, -ae, *f.* — *daughter*
5. saltō, -āre, -āvī, -ātum — *dance*
6. rogō, -āre, -āvī, -ātum — *ask*
7. ante (prep. w/acc.) — *before*
8. circum (prep. w/acc.) — *around, about*
9. superbē — *proudly*
10. horreum, -ī, *n.* — *barn*
11. līmō, -āre, -āvī, -ātum — *polish*
12. habeō, -ēre, -uī, -itum — *have, hold*
13. vestis, vestis, *f.* — *clothing, garment*
14. prīmus, -a, -um — *first*
15. gestō, -āre, -āvī, -ātum — *wear*

 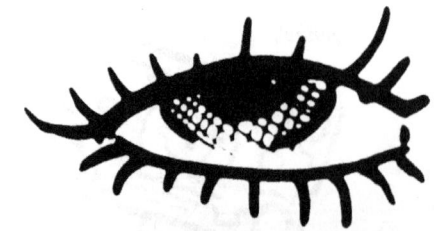

List Fourteen

DEMONSTRATIVE CHANT: IS, EA, ID

Memorize the new pronoun chant below. It can mean *this, these* or *that, those*.

SINGULAR: THIS, THAT

Masculine	Feminine	Neuter
is	ea	id
eius	eius	eius
eī	eī	eī
eum	eam	id
eō	eā	eō

PLURAL: THESE, THOSE

Masculine	Feminine	Neuter
eī	eae	ea
eōrum	eārum	eōrum
eīs	eīs	eīs
eōs	eās	ea
eīs	eīs	eīs

NUTSHELL REVIEW

Fill in the endings and the meanings in the nutshell.

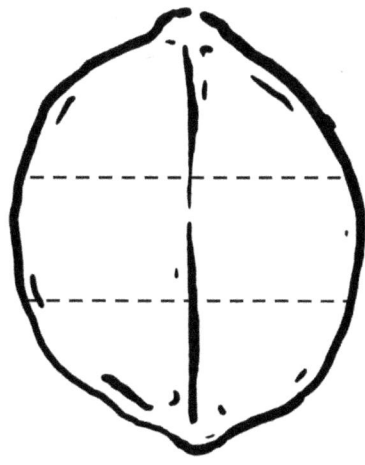

List Fourteen 241

39 Lesson Thirty-Nine

A. VERB STEM REVIEW

Fill in the blanks about finding present and perfect verb stems below.

1. To find the *present stem* of a first or second conjugation verb, remove the _____ ending from the _____ principal part of the verb.

2. What is the present stem for the first conjugation verb *numerō*? _____

3. What is the present stem for the second conjugation verb *mereō*? _____

4. To find the *present stem* of a third conjugation verb, remove the _____ ending from the _____ principal part of the verb.

5. What is the present stem for the third conjugation verb *cadō*? _____

6. To find the *perfect stem* of a first, second, or third conjugation verb, remove the _____ ending from the _____ principal part of the verb.

7. Give the *perfect stems* for the verbs below.

VERB	PERFECT STEM
numerō	_____
mereō	_____
cadō	_____

B. VERB SYNOPSIS REVIEW

Fill in the verb synopses below. Be sure to use the correct verb stem.

numerō in third person plural

TENSE	SYNOPSIS	TRANSLATION
present		
imperfect		
future		
perfect		
pluperfect		

mereō in third person plural

TENSE	SYNOPSIS	TRANSLATION
present		
imperfect		
future		
perfect		
pluperfect		

cadō in third person plural

TENSE	SYNOPSIS	TRANSLATION
present		
imperfect		
future		
perfect		
pluperfect		

C. TRANSLATE

Label and translate these sentences. Some sentences are in English and need to be translated into Latin.

1. The farmer was having a party. _____

_____

2. Convīvium erat saltātiō in horreō. _____

_____

3. Agricola illōs adulēscentēs et hās virginēs invītāverat sd saltātiōnem. _____

_____

4. Julia and Claudia were wearing pretty dresses and new shoes. _____

_____

5. Saxum caput limāvit ante convīvium. _____

_____

Lesson Thirty-Nine 245

6. Iūlius ceciderat et lāc effūderat in veste Claudī!

D. DERIVATIVE DIGGING
List at least five English verbs which begin with the prefix *de-*. *De-* comes from the Latin preposition *dē* (down from, from, about, concerning).

40 Lesson Forty

A. LINKING VERB REVIEW
Label and translate the Pattern 4 & 5 sentences below.

1. Iūlius adulēscēns erit. _____

2. Iūlia et Claudia sunt virginēs. _____
_____

3. Nova stola Iūliae est bella. _____

4. Erāmus agricolae. _____

5. Tū es lactaria. _____

B. TRANSLATE
Label and translate these sentences containing the verb *possum* and infinitives.

1. Possum vaccam mulgēre. _____

2. Potesne pecūniam merēre? _____
_____

3. Iūlius et Cladius nōn possunt pullōs parvōs gallīnae numerāre. _____
_____

4. Quīs potest saltātiōnem prīmam saltāre? _____
_____

C. ABLATIVE OF PLACE "WHERE"

Give Latin answers to the following questions about the location of a person or thing. Use the Latin preposition *in (meaning in or on)* followed by a place in the ablative case. Use any vocabulary words we have studied this year. One is done as an example.

1. Ubī est lāc?   *Lāc est in mulctrā.*

2. Ubī est agricola? _____

3. Ubī est calceus Claudi? _____

4. Ubī est convīvium Claudiae? _____

_____

5. Ubī est pecūnia Iūlī? _____

6. Ubī sunt līberī et Saxum? _____

_____

D. DERIVATIVE DIGGING

Choose a derivative from List 14 and write its etymology on the lines below.

Word: _____

Etymology: _____

_____

_____

248 Lesson Forty

41 Lesson Forty-One

A. DEMONSTRATIVE ADJECTIVE REVIEW: HIC & ILLE
Fill in missing parts of the demonstrative adjectives *hic* and *ille*.

Hic, etc. means _____

Masculine	Feminine	Neuter
hic		hoc
	huius	
		huic
hunc		
	hāc	

Hi, etc. means _____

Masculine	Feminine	Neuter
		haec
hōrum		
	hīs	
		haec
hīs		

Ille, etc. means _____

Masculine	Feminine	Neuter
	illa	
		illius
illī		
	illam	
		illō

Illi, etc. means _____

Masculine	Feminine	Neuter
illī		
	illārum	
		illīs
illōs		
	illīs	

B. TRANSLATE

Translate the following phrases into Latin. You will be told what case to use. Pay attention to the gender and number.

1. this young woman (nominative) _____

2. those shoes (accusative) _____

3. these chicks (dative) _____

4. that milkmaid's (genitive) _____

5. this market (ablative) _____

Lesson Forty-One

6. that milk (nominative) _____

7. these young men's (genitive) _____

Challenge: those farmers (accusative) _____

C. IMPERATIVE REVIEW

Circle the correct answers in the statements about imperatives (commands). Look at Lessons 5A, Unit 1 Review Section A, and Lesson 14C for review.

1. The present tense verb stem can also be used as:

   a. a singular command

   b. a plural command

   c. a question

2. Which principal part of the verb is used to find the present stem for first and second conjugation verbs?

   a. the first part

   b. the second part

   c. the fourth part

3. What ending is added to the present stem to form a plural command for first and second conjugation verbs?

   a. -re

   b. -ne

   c. -te

4. Which principal part of the verb is used to find the present stem for third conjugation verbs?

   a. the first part

   b. the second part

   c. the fourth part

5. What ending is added to the present stem to form a singular command for third conjugation verbs?

   a. -ō

   b. -tis

   c. -e

6. What ending is added to the present stem to form a plural command for third conjugation verbs?

   a. -ite

   b. -te

   c. -ete

D. WRITE LATIN COMMANDS

Write Latin commands using verbs from Lists 13 and 14 and then translate your commands. Pay attention to the conjugations of the verbs you choose. They can be singular or plural commands. Perhaps your teacher will let you give some commands to your classmates to act out. One is done for you.

LATIN COMMAND	TRANSLATION
1. Ne* effunde lāc.	*Don't spill the milk.*
2. _____	_____
3. _____	_____
4. _____	_____

E. POSSESSIVE ADJECTIVE MEUS, MEA, MEUM (MY)

When you want to show that something belongs to you in Latin, you use the possessive adjective *meus, mea, meum*, which means "my." Like other adjectives, the possessive adjective must match the noun it describes in gender, number, and case. Consider the nominative examples below:

   meus pullus *(my chick)*   mea vacca *(my cow)*   meum ōvum *(my egg)*

Decline the noun-possessive adjective phrases on the following page. Some parts have been filled in for you.

N.B. When more than one adjective describes a single noun, the adjectives may be connected by the conjunction *et (and)*. See the example below. Note the two possible translations.

   Claudia stolam novam et rosam emit.   *Claudia buys a new pink dress.*
   Claudia buys a new and pink dress.

* *Ne* makes a negative command.

252 Lesson Forty-One

MASCULINE

	Singular	Plural
Nom.	pullus meus	
Gen.		pullōrum meōrum
Dat.		pullīs meīs
Acc.	pullum meum	
Abl.	pullō meō	

FEMININE

	Singular	Plural
Nom.	vacca mea	vaccae meae
Gen.	vaccae meae	
Dat.	vaccae meae	
Acc.		vaccās meās
Abl.		

NEUTER

	Singular	Plural
Nom.	ōvum meum	ōva mea
Gen.	ōvī meī	
Dat.		
Acc.		
Abl.	ōvō meō	ōvīs meīs

Lesson Forty-One

42 Lesson Forty-Two
The Milkmaid & Her Pail

Translate the fable of *The Milkmaid and Her Pail*. You do not have to label unless you are having difficulty translating a sentence.

1. Ōlim lactaria vaccam mulgēbat. _____

2. Lactaria erat filia agricolae. _____

3. Complēvit mulctram et lāc portāvit in capite. _____

4. Lactaria ambulāvit in viā ad macellum lāc vēnditāre. _____

5. Dum ambulābat, lactaria putābat dē pecūniā. _____

6. "Vēndītābō lāc," inquit, "et emam ōva multa." _____

7. "Ōva exclūdent et multōs pullōs habēbō." _____

Lesson Forty-Two 255

8. "Pullī erunt gallīnae et gallīnae ōva parient." _____

9. "Vēndītābō ōva et pecūnia mea augēbit." _____

10. "Emam stolam novam et bellam* gestam eam in saltātiōne." _____

11. "Adulēscentēs meās genās roseās et meōs gradus** flavōs, et meōs oculōs caeruleōs spectābunt." _____

12. "Virginēs meam stolam novam et bellam vidēbunt." _____

13. "Multī adulēscentēs saltātiōnēs multās saltāre mē rogābunt," lactaria cōgitāvit. _____

14. Tum lactaria caput quassit superbē. _____

15. Mulctra cecidit dē capite lactariae! _____

* *New, beautiful.*
** *Gradus is fourth declension accusative plural in this sentence.*

256 Lesson Forty-Two

16. Lāc effudit humī. _____

_____

17. Somnia lactariae ēvānuit! _____

_____

18. "Ego sum," inquit, "stulta lactaria." _____

_____

Morum praeceptum: Pullos ne numerā ante exclūduntur.
(Don't count your chickens before they are hatched.)

N.B. Possessive pronouns are often implied in Latin. Sentence 14 is a good example. Although no possessive adjective is given in the Latin, what possessive pronoun would make sense in your English translation?

FABLE GLOSSARY

1. ambulō, -āre, -āvī, -ātum	*walk*
2. portō, -āre, -āvī, -ātum	*carry*
3. compleō, -ēre, -plēvī, -plētum	*fill, fill up*
4. gestō, -āre, -āvī, -ātum	*wear*
5. ēvānēscō, -ere, ēvānuī,———	*vanish, disappear*
6. inquit	*he, she, it said*
7. via, -ae, *f.*	*road*
8. humus, -ī, *f.*	*ground*
9. somnium, -ī, *n.*	*a dream*
10. dum	*while*
11. tum	*then*
12. dē	*down from*
13. meus, -a, -um	*my*
14. stultus, -a, -um	*foolish*
15. mē (from Ego Chant)	*me*
16. cōgitō, -āre, -āvī, -ātum	*think*
17. ōlim	*once (once upon a time)*

Unit Seven Review

A. LATIN FLOWERS

Draw a Latin flower with a *present stem*. Then add three layers of petals for the present, imperfect, and future tense verb endings for first and second conjugation verbs. Next to this flower, draw another flower with a present stem, but this time add three layers of petals (present, imperfect, and future tense endings) for *third* conjugation verbs.

Now draw a Latin flower with a perfect stem. Add two layers of petals for the perfect and pluperfect endings. These endings are the same for all three verb conjugations.

Unit Seven Review

B. VERB SYNOPSIS

Do a verb synopsis for the third conjugation verb *exclūdō, -ere, -clūsī, -clūsum* in the first person plural.

TENSE	SYNOPSIS	TRANSLATION
present		
imperfect		
future		
perfect		

C. VERB PRACTICE

Translate the verbs below. Identify the conjugation.

VERB	TRANSLATION	CONJUGATION
1. mulget		
2. dormītābant		
3. ēmerās		
4. numerāveram		
5. cecidī		
6. merēbit		
7. pepererant		
8. quassistis		
9. dormītāverāmus		
10. cadam		

Challenge:

VERB	TRANSLATION	CONJUGATION
effundit	_____	_____
effūdit	_____	_____
effundet	_____	_____

D. LINKING VERB PRACTICE

Translate the linking verb forms below. Remember, linking verbs *stand alone*.

1. estis _____

2. erō _____

3. erātis _____

4. erat _____

5. sunt _____

E. TRANSLATING COMMANDS

Translate these commands into Latin, giving both the singular command and the plural command. Pay attention to the conjugation of the verb. One is done as an example.

	SINGULAR COMMAND	PLURAL COMMAND
1. Buy eggs.	Eme ōva.	Emite ōva.
2. Sell the cow.	_____	_____
3. Earn money.	_____	_____
4. Shut out the chickens.	_____	_____

Unit Seven Review

F. SENTENCE TRANSLATION

Label and translate the sentences below. Especially watch for the demonstrative adjectives *hic* and *ille*, the possessive adjective *meus*, and a series of adjectives describing a noun, which are connected with the conjunction *et*.

1. Iūlius hōs pullōs numerāverat sed Claudius illōs pullōs numerābit. _____

2. "Possum," Claudia inquit, "vaccam meam mulgēre." _____

3. "Pullī meī," Iūlia inquit, "nōn possunt ōva parere." _____

4. Saxum vestēs novōs et bellōs ante convīvium ēmerat. _____

G. DERIVATIVE PARAGRAPH

Write a short paragraph using ten derivatives from Lists 13 and 14. <u>Underline</u> the derivatives.

Unit Seven Review

Unit 8

List Fifteen

VOCABULARY

Memorize the following Latin words and their translations. Learn the principal parts of the verbs and the genitive and gender of the nouns.

WORD	DERIVATIVE	TRANSLATION
1. ūnus	_____	*one*
2. duo	_____	*two*
3. trēs	_____	*three*
4. quattuor	_____	*four*
5. quinque	_____	*five*
6. sex	_____	*six*
7. septem	_____	*seven*
8. octō	_____	*eight*
9. novem	_____	*nine*
10. decem	_____	*ten*
11. centum	_____	*a hundred*
12. mille	_____	*a thousand*
13. numerus, -ī, *m.*	_____	*number*

WORD	DERIVATIVE	TRANSLATION
14. respōnsum, -ī, *n.*	_____	*an answer, response*
15. addō, -ere, -didī, -ditum	_____	*add*
16. dēdūcō, -ere, -dūxī, -ductum	_____	*substract*
17. multiplicō, -āre, -āvī, -ātum	_____	*multiply*
18. dīvido, -ere, -vīsī, -vīsum	_____	*divide*
19. respondeō, -ēre, respondī, respōnsum	_____	*respond, answer*
20. quot (indeclinable adj.)	_____	*how many?*

REVIEW WORDS

1. schola, -ae, *f.* — *classroom*
2. magister, -tri, *m.* — *teacher*
3. magistra, -ae, *f.* — *female teacher*
4. scrībō, -ere, scrīpsī, scrīptum — *write*
5. mensa, -ae, *f.* — *desk, table*
6. lūdus, -ī, *m.* — *school*
7. arithmētica, -ae, *f.* — *arithmetic*
8. numerō, -āre, -āvī, -ātum — *count*
9. rogō, -āre, -āvī, -ātum — *ask*
10. inquit — *he, she, it said* (used with quotations)

RELATIVE PRONOUN CHANT

Memorize the relative pronoun chant below. It means *who* or *which*.

SINGULAR: WHO, WHICH

Masculine	Feminine	Neuter
quī	quae	quod
cuius	cuius	cuius
cui	cui	cui
quem	quam	quod
quō	quā	quō

PLURAL: WHO, WHICH

Masculine	Feminine	Neuter
quī	quae	quae
quōrum	quārum	quōrum
quibus	quibus	quibus
quōs	quās	quae
quibus	quibus	quibus

43 Lesson Forty-Three

A. ROMAN NUMERALS REVIEW

Write the correct Roman numeral next to the Latin numbers below.
Roman numerals: I, II, III, IV, V, VI, VII, VIII, IX, X

LATIN NUMBER	ROMAN NUMERAL
1. trēs	_____
2. sex	_____
3. novem	_____
4. ūnus	_____
5. quinque	_____
6. octō	_____
7. decem	_____
8. duo	_____
9. quattuor	_____
10. septem	_____

B. ADJECTIVE/NOUN AGREEMENT: NUMBERS ARE SPECIAL

Adjectives must match the nouns they describe in *gender, number* and *case*. This is true of the cardinal numbers *ūnus, duo,* and *trēs* as well. While all numbers are adjectives, only these three must match the nouns they describe. The other numbers do not change their endings. In this book we will only be concerned with the nominative and accusative cases. Consider the following examples.

NOMINATIVE

Masculine		Feminine		Neuter	
ūnus puer	*one boy*	ūna puella	*one girl*	ūnum saxum	*one rock*
duo puerī	*two boys*	duae puellae	*two girls*	duo saxa	*two rocks*
trēs puerī	*three boys*	trēs puellae	*three girls*	tria saxa	*three rocks*

ACCUSATIVE

Masculine		Feminine		Neuter	
ūnum puerum	*one boy*	ūnam puellam	*one girl*	ūnum saxum	*one rock*
duōs puerōs	*two boys*	duās puellās	*two girls*	duō saxa	*two rocks*
trēs puerōs	*three boys*	trēs puellās	*three girls*	tria saxa	*three rocks*

N.B. You do not need to *decline* (change endings) for numbers above three.

septem puerī	*seven boys* (nominative)
septem puerōs	*seven boys* (accusative)
octō puellae	*eight girls* (nominative)
octō puellās	*eight girls* (accusative)
quattuor saxa	*four rocks* (nominative)
quattuor saxa	*four rocks* (accusative)

C. TRANSLATE

Label and translate the sentences below.

1. Iūlia trēs numerōs citō multiplicābat. _____

_____

2. Magister rogat, "Quot puellae in hāc scholā sunt?" _____

_____

Lesson Forty-Three

3. Ūnus discipulus et duae puellae magistrum respondērunt. _____

_____

_____

4. "Sunt," inquiunt,* "trēs puellae in hāc scholā." _____

_____

5. "Et habēmus," inquit Iūlius, "ūnum Saxum!" _____

_____

6. "Quot puerōs," rogāvit magister, "habēmus in scholā?" _____

_____

7. Claudia magistrum respondit, "Habēmus duōs puerōs." _____

_____

D. DERIVATIVE DIGGING

Brainstorm a list of derivatives from the Latin number *ūnus* and write them on the lines below. Then look up the meaning of one of them and write its definition.

ūnus: _____

_____

Derivative: _____

Definition: _____

_____

* *Inquiunt* means "they said."

Lesson Forty-Three

44 Lesson Forty-Four

A. TRANSLATE
Translate the sentences below. Where called for, answer the math questions in Latin.

1. Discipulī numerōs multōs addunt, dēdūcunt, multiplicant, et dīvidunt in scholā. _____

2. Magister Iūlium rogat, "Quot sunt trēs et quattuor?" _____

3. Claudia decem et centum multiplicat. _____

4. Iūlia mille dīvidit ā decem. _____

5. Claudius duo ā quīnque dēdūcit. _____

6. Magister discipulōs imperat, "Multiplicāte hōs numerōs sed dīvidite illōs numerōs." _____

Now give the correct answer to the Latin math questions above. One is done as an example.

1. "Quot sunt trēs et quattuor?" Quid est respōnsum Iūliī? _____*septem*_____

2. Claudia decem et centum multiplicat. Quid est respōnsum Claudiae? _____

3. Iulia mille dīvidit ā decem. Quid est responsum Iūliae? _____

4. Claudius duo ā quinque dēdūcit. Quid est responsum Claudiī? _____

B. POSSESSIVE ADJECTIVE TUUS, TUA, TUUM

We have learned the first person singular possessive adjective *meus, mea, meum* which means *my*. Now we will learn to use the second person singular adjective, *tuus, tua, tuum* which means *your*.
Remember that possessive adjectives must match the nouns they describe in *gender*, *number*, and *case* just like any other adjective. With that in mind, decline the noun-adjective phrases below.

MASCULINE: *your school*

	Singular	Plural
Nom.	lūdus tuus	
Gen.	lūdī tuī	
Dat.		
Acc.		
Abl.		

FEMININE: *your desk*

	Singular	Plural
Nom.	mensa tua	
Gen.	mensae tuae	
Dat.		
Acc.		
Abl.		

NEUTER: *your answer*

	Singular	Plural
Nom.	responsum tuum	
Gen.	responsī tuī	
Dat.		
Acc.		
Abl.		

C. REVIEW OF CARDINAL NUMBERS ONE, TWO & THREE

Translate the noun-adjective phrases below into Latin in the nominative and accusative cases. Remember that the numbers *ūnus, duo, and trēs* must match the nouns they describe in gender, number and case. Higher numbers do not decline.

PHRASE	NOMINATIVE	ACCUSATIVE
1. one male teacher	*ūnus magister*	*ūnum magistrum*
2. three answers		
3. two schools		
4. five classrooms		
5. seven desks		

D. ETYMOLOGY

Choose a derivative from the Latin numbers on List 15. Look up the etymology of your derivative and write it on the lines below.

Derivative: _____

Etymology: _____

_____

Lesson Forty-Four

 # List Sixteen

A. VOCABULARY

Memorize the following Latin words and their translations. Learn the principal parts of the verbs and the genitive and gender of nouns.

WORD	DERIVATIVE	TRANSLATION
1. prīmus, -a, -um	_____	*first*
2. secundus, -a, -um	_____	*second*
3. tertius, -a, -um	_____	*third*
4. quārtus, -a, -um	_____	*fourth*
5. quīntus, -a, -um	_____	*fifth*
6. sextus, -a, -um	_____	*sixth*
7. septimus, -a, -um	_____	*seventh*
8. octāvus, -a, -um	_____	*eighth*
9. nōnus, -a, -um	_____	*ninth*
10. decimus, -a, -um	_____	*tenth*
11. ānser, ānseris, *m.*	_____	*goose*
12. diēs, diēī, *m.**	_____	*day*

* From fifth declension

WORD	DERIVATIVE	TRANSLATION
13. nox, noctis, *f.*	_____	*night*
14. hōra, -ae, *f.*	_____	*hour*
15. mēnsis, -is, *m.*	_____	*month*
16. annus, -ī, *m.*	_____	*year*
17. tempus, temporis, *n.*	_____	*time*
18. avārus, -a, -um	_____	*greedy*
19. quandō (interrogative)	_____	*when?*
20. intrā (prep. w/acc.)	_____	*inside*

REVIEW WORDS

1. studeō, -ēre, -uī, ——**   *study*
2. legō, -ere, lēgī, lēctum   *read*
3. arithmētica, -ae, *f.*   *arithmetic*
4. historia, -ae, *f.*   *history*
5. geōgraphia, -ae, *f.*   *geography*
6. liber, librī, *m.*   *book*
7. adiūdicō, -āre, -āvī, -ātum   *award*
8. praemium, -ī, *n.*   *prize*
9. celebrō, -āre, -āvī, -ātum   *celebrate*
10. diēs natālis, diēī natālis, *m.*   *birthday*
11. mūsica, -ae, *f.*   *music*
12. nunc (adv.)   *now*

** *Studeo* does not usually take a direct object in the accusative case. Instead, the direct object is put in the *dative* case.

List Sixteen

45 Lesson Forty-Five

A. PERFECT & PLUPERFECT VERB TENSE REVIEW

Conjugate and translate the verb *respondeō* in the perfect and pluperfect tenses. Write the principal parts and the perfect stem of the verb *respondeō*. Then conjugate and translate.

principal parts: *respondeō*, _____, _____, _____.

perfect stem: _____

PERFECT TENSE

PLUPERFECT TENSE

Now we will learn the *future perfect verb tense*, whose endings also are attached to the perfect stem:

FUTURE PERFECT VERB TENSE ENDINGS

-erō – *I will have*	-erimus – *we will have*
-eris – *you will have*	-eritis – *you all will have*
-erit – *he, she, it will have*	-erint – *they will have*

Attached to the perfect stem are the perfect, pluperfect, and future perfect endings.

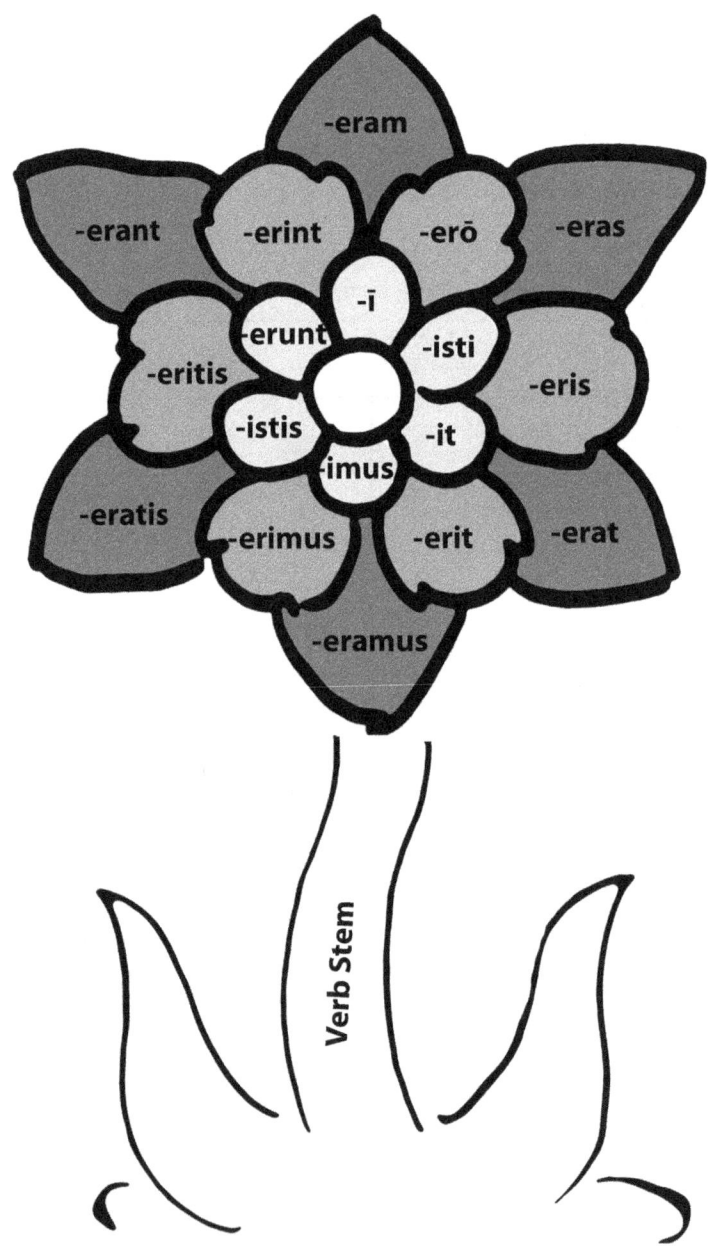

282 Lesson Forty-Five

B. PRACTICE

Underline endings and practice translating verbs from the perfect, pluperfect, and future perfect tenses. One set is done as an example.

1. multiplicāv<u>it</u>   *he, she, it multiplied (has multiplied, did multiply)*

   multiplicāv<u>erat</u>   *he, she, it had multiplied*

   multiplicāv<u>erit</u>   *he, she, it will have multiplied*

2. dēdūximus   _____

   deduxerāmus   _____

   dēdūxerimus   _____

3. addidērunt   _____

   addiderant   _____

   addiderint   _____

4. dīvisī   _____

   dīviseram   _____

   dīviserō   _____

5. respondistī   _____

   responderās   _____

   responderis   _____

6. scrīpsistis   _____

   scrīpserātis   _____

   scrīpseritis   _____

C. TRANSLATE
Label and translate these sentences.

1. Duo discipulī novī et duae discipulae novae in scholā sunt. _____

2. Discipulī arithmēticae* studuērunt. _____

3. Claudius historiam Romae lēgerit. _____

4. Iūlia amāverat geōgraphiae* studēre. _____

5. Magistra Saxō prīmum praemium adiūdicāverat in musicā! _____

Challenge sentence: Discipulī diem nātālis Claudiae celebrāverint in mēnse septimō. _____

D. PREPOSITIONS & PREFIXES
Use an English dictionary to look up one of these words which begins with the prefix *intra-*.
Write your word and its definition on the lines provided.
Word choices: *intradermal, intramolecular, intramural, intramuscular, intratelluric, intravenous*

Word: _____

* Remember that *studeo* usually requires a direct object in the dative case!

Lesson Forty-Five

Definition: _____
_____
_____

46 Lesson Forty-Six

A. FUTURE PERFECT TENSE REVIEW
Fill in the future perfect tense endings and meanings in the box below.

FUTURE PERFECT VERB TENSE

-erō –	

B. SYNOPSIS REVIEW
Do synopses for the verbs below. Also identify the conjugation of each verb.

Multiplicō, multiplicāre, multiplicāvī, multiplicātum in first person plural:

Conjugation? _____

TENSE	SYNOPSIS	TRANSLATION
present		
imperfect		
future		
perfect		
pluperfect		
future perfect		

Respondeō, respondēre, respondī, respōnsum in second person singular:

Conjugation? _____

TENSE	SYNOPSIS	TRANSLATION
present		
imperfect		
future		
perfect		
pluperfect		
future perfect		

Dīvidō, dīvidere, dīvisī, dīvisum in third person singular:

Conjugation? _____

TENSE	SYNOPSIS	TRANSLATION
present		
imperfect		
future		
perfect		
pluperfect		
future perfect		

C. ABLATIVE OF TIME "WHEN" & ABLATIVE OF TIME "DURING"

When speaking of a specific time, the ablative case is used without a preposition. This is called the **ablative of time "when."** The ablative of time when is used with ordinal numbers to tell time. Study the example below.

    Iūlia tertiā horā ad ludum ambulāvit.   *Julia walked to school at the third hour.*

When speaking of a time during which something occurs, the ablative case is also used without a preposition. This is called the **ablative of time "within which."**

    Iūlius quīntā horā arithmēticae studēbat.   *Julius was studying arithmetic at the fifth hour.*

D. TRANSLATE
Label and translate the sentences below.

1. Līberī secundā hōrā fābulās legēbant. _____

2. Magister imperat, "Nunc, scrībite fābulās dē ānsere ōvis* aureīs." _____

3. "Claudia," magister inquit, "quartā hōrā fābulam tuam lege." _____

4. Līberī fābulam Claudiae auscultant. _____

Challenge: Now answer the questions below in Latin using complete sentences.

1. Quandō līberī fābulās legēbant? _____

* Be careful! Is *ōvīs* from *ovis* or *ōvum*?

Lesson Forty-Six

2. Quandō Claudia fābulam lēgit? _____

_____

E. DERIVATIVE DIGGING

Choose a derivative from List 16 and write its meaning on the lines below. Then use your derivative in a sentence.

Derivative: _____

Definition: _____

_____

Sentence: _____

_____

47 Lesson Forty-Seven

A. ORDINAL & CARDINAL NUMBER PRACTICE
Translate the following noun-adjective phrases into Latin. All are in the nominative case.

1. the first goose _____

2. one goose _____

3. seven months _____

4. the seventh month _____

5. three hours _____

6. the third hour _____

7. two rocks _____

8. the second rock _____

9. ten desks _____

10. the tenth desk _____

B. POSSESSIVE ADJECTIVE PRACTICE
Label and translate the sentences below containing the possessive pronouns *my* (meus, -a, -um) and *your* (tuus, -a, -um) into Latin. Be sure to make *meus* and *tuus* agree with the nouns they describe in gender, number, and case.

1. My goose lays eggs, but your goose does not lay eggs. _____

_____

2. The teacher writes my answer on the board, but he does not write your answer. _____

_____

_____

3. Books are inside my desk, but your desk does not have books. _____

_____

C. ABLATIVE OF TIME REVIEW
Translate the sentences below.

1. Julia will add the numbers at the third hour. _____

_____

2. Julius and Saxum were counting the geese during the hour. _____

_____

48 Lesson Forty-Eight
The Goose That Laid the Golden Egg

Translate the fable below.

1. Ōlim erat vir pauperculus. _____

2. Cum uxōre in casā habitābat. _____

3. Vir et uxor nullam pecūniam habuērunt. _____

4. Vir aliēnus repente apparuit! _____

5. Vir aliēnus virō pauperculō ānserem fēminam dedit. _____

6. "Cūrā ānserem fēminam meam," inquit, "et ānser femina te curābit." _____

7. Vir alienus ēvānuit. _____

8. Vir et uxor ānserī fēminae nīdum fēcerunt et ānserī fēminae cibum et aquam dederunt. _____

9. Mane erat ōvum aureum intrā nidum! _____

10. Vir et uxor ōvum aureum vēndītāvērunt et potuērunt cibum emere. _____

11. Cotīdiē ānser fēmina ōvum peperit. _____

12. Mox vir et uxor multam pecūniam habēbant. _____

13. Iam vir et uxor erant avārī. _____

14. Uxor rogāvit, "Quot ōva intrā ānserem fēminam sunt?" _____

15. Ānserem fēminam interfēcērunt sed nūlla ōva aurea intrā ānserem fēminam erant. _____

16. Vir aliēnus ambulāvit in casam. _____

17. "Vōs* estis," inquit, "stultī et avārī." _____

* You (plural)

Lesson Forty-Eight

18. Vir aliēnus et ānser fēmina mortua ēvānuerunt! _____

_____

Morum praeceptum: Este grāti, nōn avārī. *(Be thankful, not greedy.)*

FABLE GLOSSARY

1. ānser femina — *female goose*
2. vir, virī, *m.* — *man or husband*
3. uxor, uxōris, *f.* — *wife*
4. pauperculus, -a, -um — *poor*
5. nullus, -a, -um — *no*
6. casa, -ae, *f.* — *cottage*
7. nīdus, -ī, *m.* — *nest*
8. ōvum, -ī, *m.* — *egg*
9. aliēnus, -a, -um — *strange, foreign*
10. aureus, -a, -um — *golden*
11. avārus, -a, -um — *greedy*
12. stultus, -a, -um — *foolish*
13. ēvānēscō, -ere, ēvānui, —— — *vanish*
14. pariō, parere, peperī, partum — *bear, bring forth (w/ōva=lay eggs)*
15. habitō, -āre, -āvī, -ātum — *live in*
16. curō, -āre, -āvī, -ātum — *care for*
17. interficiō, -ere, -fēcī, -fectum — *kill*
18. habeō, -ere, habuī, habitum — *have, hold*
19. appareō, -ere, apparuī, apparitum — *appear*
20. mane — *in the morning*
21. repente — *suddenly*
22. cotidiē — *every day*
23. mox — *soon*
24. iam — *now*
25. faciō, facere, fēcī, factum — *make*
26. potuerunt — *they were able*
27. cum — *with*
28. mortuus, -a, -um — *dead*

Tē and *vōs* are from the personal pronoun chant.

Lesson Forty-Eight

Unit Eight Review

A. CARDINAL AND ORDINAL NUMBER REVIEW
Translate the noun-adjective phrases below into Latin. Both cardinal and ordinal numbers are used. All are in the nominative case.

1. one day _____

2. the first hour _____

3. the sixth month _____

4. six months _____

5. the fourth time _____

6. three geese _____

7. two geese _____

8. ten geese _____

9. the second night _____

10. two nights _____

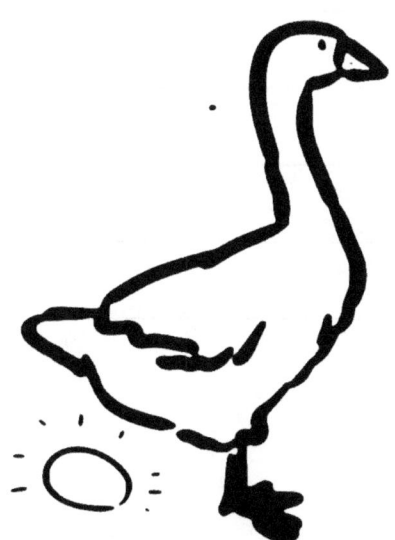

B. NOUN-ADJECTIVE AGREEMENT
Decline the noun-adjective phrase *your prize*.

CASE	SINGULAR	PLURAL
Nom.	praemium tuum	
Gen.		
Dat.		
Acc.		
Abl.		

C. FUTURE PERFECT TENSE REVIEW
Write out the future perfect verb tense endings and meanings in the paradigm below:

FUTURE PERFECT VERB TENSE ENDINGS

-erō –	

D. LINKING VERB PRACTICE
Translate the present, imperfect, and future tense linking verbs below.

1. erāmus _____

2. sunt _____

3. eritis _____

4. es _____

5. erat _____

6. erunt _____

E. VERB SYNOPSIS PRACTICE

Find the verb stems and do a verb synopsis for the third conjugation verb *addō, addere, addidī, additum* in the second person plural.

present stem: _____ perfect stem: _____

TENSE	SYNOPSIS	TRANSLATION
present		
imperfect		
future		
perfect		
pluperfect		
future perfect		

Find the verb stems and do a verb synopsis for the first conjugation verb *multiplico, -āre, -āvī, -ātum* in the third person singular.

present stem: _____ perfect stem: _____

TENSE	SYNOPSIS	TRANSLATION
present		
imperfect		
future		
perfect		
pluperfect		
future perfect		

Unit Eight Review

F. ABLATIVE OF TIME PRACTICE
Translate these sentences containing ablatives of time:

1. Saxum quinque fābulās mēnse leget. _____

2. Magister praemium prīmum hōrā nōnā adiudicābit. _____

G. SENTENCE TRANSLATION
Label and translate these sentences.

1. Septem ānserēs arithmēticam diē studuerint. _____

2. Iūlius mille numerōs annō addiderat. _____

3. Claudia et Iūlia magistrō respōnsum dedērunt. _____

Challenge Sentence:

My teacher multiplies numbers in the third hour, but your teacher divided numbers at the second hour.

H. ANSWERING QUESTIONS
Answer the questions below in complete Latin sentences.

1. Quot ānserēs arithmēticam studuerint? _____

_____

2. Quandō Iūlius mille numerōs addiderat? _____

_____

I. DERIVATIVE REVIEW
Give derivatives for the words below.

1. centum _____ 6. prīmus _____

2. dēdūcō _____ 7. decimus _____

3. quattuor _____ 8. nox _____

4. ūnus _____ 9. avārus _____

5. numerus _____ 10. intrā _____

Unit Eight Review 301

Unit 9

49 Lesson Forty-Nine
Review: Lists 1-6 & Units 1-3

A. VOCABULARY
Read through Lists 1–6 and translate as many of the following words as you can from memory. Then look up any you don't remember.

1. Graecia _____

2. fābula _____

3. nōn _____

4. grēx _____

5. mendācium _____

6. curriculum _____

7. praemium _____

8. somnus _____

9. auris _____

10. arbor _____

11. epistula _____

12. nux _____

13. cibus _____

14. mūs _____

15. ubī _____

16. narrātor _____

17. vīcus _____

18. pastor _____

19. liber _____

20. vēritās _____

21. arbiter _____

22. cunīculus _____

23. sub (prep. w/abl.) _____

24. via _____

25. testūdo _____

26. coquus _____

27. cēna _____

28. fēles _____

29. marītus _____

30. angulus _____

B. FINDING THE PRESENT STEM
Fill in the blanks about how to find the present verb stem.

First and Second Conjugation

To find the present stem, go to the _____ principal part of the verb, remove the ending _____ .

Third Conjugation

To find the present stem, go to the _____ principal part of the verb, remove the ending _____ .

C. THIRD CONJUGATION PRESENT & FUTURE TENSES
Fill in the *third conjugation* verb endings in the boxes below. Translate endings.

PRESENT TENSE

-ō –	

FUTURE TENSE

-am –	

D. VERB TRANSLATION & CONJUGATION IDENTIFICATION
Translate the verbs below. Tell whether they are first, second, or third conjugation. All are from the present, imperfect, and future tenses only.

VERB   **TRANSLATION**   **CONJUGATION**

1. oppugnābit _____   _____

2. terrēbāmus _____   _____

VERB	TRANSLATION	CONJUGATION

3. contendent _____ _____

4. currunt _____ _____

5. scrībētis _____ _____

6. volātis _____ _____

7. legit _____ _____

8. ēdam _____ _____

9. pōtābam _____ _____

10. occultās _____ _____

11. rīdēbās _____ _____

12. lūdunt _____ _____

E. IMPERATIVE REVIEW

Translate these first and second conjugation commands into Latin. Pay attention to whether the command is singular or plural.

1. Train the dolphin. (singular) _____

2. Train the runner. (plural) _____

3. Wait for the tortoise. (singular) _____

4. Wait for dessert. (plural) _____

Now translate these third conjugation commands.

5. Eat the apple. (singular) _____

6. Eat dessert. (plural) _____

F. SENTENCE PATTERNS 4 & 5
Label and translate the Pattern 4 and Pattern 5 sentences below.

1. Iūlia et Claudia vīcinae sunt. _____

2. Canis nōn erat fēles. _____

3. Nūcleī nucēs erunt. _____

4. Claudius est citus. _____

G. SENTENCE & QUESTIONS TRANSLATION
Label and translate the sentences and questions below.

1. Curretne testūdō curriculum longum? _____

2. Eritne cunīculus superbus victor? _____

3. Ubī erātis? _____

4. Sub arbōribus erāmus. _____

5. Excitābuntne līberī vulpem dēfessam? _____

6. Puer vēritātem nōn narrābat sed mendācium narrābat. _____

Lesson Forty-Nine

7. Pastor bonus ovēs Iuliī exspectat. _____

8. Julius will write Julia a letter. _____

H. DECLENSION EXAMPLES

Give an example for each of the noun declensions below. Give both the nominative and genitive singular forms. Choose nouns from Lists 1–6.

1. first declension _____

2. second declension _____

3. second declension neuter _____

4. third declension _____

I. CONJUGATION EXAMPLES

Give an example of each of the verb conjugations below. List the first and second principal parts. Choose verbs from Lists 1–6.

1. first conjugation _____

2. second conjugation _____

3. third conjugation _____

50 Lesson Fifty
Review: Lists 7-12 & Units 4-6

A. VOCABULARY

Read through Lists 7–12 and then translate as many of the following words as you can from memory. Look up any you don't remember.

1. nix _____

2. tempestās _____

3. folium _____

4. per (prep. w/acc) _____

5. formīca _____

6. misericordia _____

7. ferus, -a, -um _____

8. pes _____

9. corpus _____

10. grātus, -a, -um _____

11. pinna _____

12. aquila _____

13. rīvus _____

14. mundus _____

15. rīpa _____

16. ventus _____

17. gelidus, -a, -um _____

18. rēgīna _____

19. trans (prep. w/acc) _____

20. fames _____

21. leō _____

22. super (prep. w/acc) _____

23. mare _____

24. caput _____

25. silva _____

26. avis _____

27. columba _____

28. caelum _____

29. prope (prep. w/acc) _____

30. ruber, rubra, rubrum _____

Lesson Fifty 311

B. VERB CONJUGATION PRACTICE

Review the first/second conjugation verb endings in the present, imperfect and future and then compare with third conjugation verb endings by filling in the boxes below. Also give meanings.

FIRST/SECOND CONJ. PRESENT

-ō –	

FIRST/SECOND CONJ. IMPERFECT

-bam –	

FIRST/SECOND CONJ. FUTURE

-bō –	

THIRD CONJ. PRESENT

-ō –	

THIRD CONJ. IMPERFECT

-ēbam –	

THIRD CONJ. FUTURE

-am —	

C. FORMING ADVERBS

Fill in the blanks in the rule for forming adverbs from adjectives.

To form an adverb in Latin, remove the ending from the _____ (masculine, feminine,

neuter) form of the adjective and add the ending _____ .

Form adverbs from the Latin adjectives below and then translate the adverbs.

ADJECTIVE	ADVERB	TRANSLATION
1. ferus, -a, -um	_____	_____
2. grātus, -a, -um	_____	_____
3. maestus, -a, -um	_____	_____

D. THIRD DECLENSION PRACTICE

Fill in the third declension chants below.

THIRD DECLENSION

-x	
-is	

THIRD DECLENSION NEUTER

-x	
-is	

Lesson Fifty

THIRD DECLENSION I-STEM

-is	
-is	

THIRD DECLENSION I-STEM NEUTER

-x	
-is	

E. THIRD DECLENSION I-STEM RULES

Give an example noun for each of the third declension i-stem rules below. Be sure to give both the nominative and genitive singular for your examples.

RULE #1: If a noun ends in -*is* or -*es* in the nominative singular, and the nominative and genitive singular have the same number of syllables, then the noun is an i-stem.

Examples: _____, _____

RULE #2: If a noun ends in -*s* or -*x* in the nominative singular, and its base ends in two consonants, then the noun is an i-stem.

Examples: _____, _____

RULE #3: If the noun is neuter, and the nominative singular ends in -*al* or -*e,* the noun is an i-stem.

Examples: _____, _____

F. PERSONAL PRONOUN REVIEW

Fill in the personal pronoun chants below and answer questions about the Latin pronouns.

FIRST PERSON

Singular	Plural
ego	nōs

SECOND PERSON

Singular	Plural
tū	vōs

Translate the nominative forms of the personal pronoun.

ego _____   nōs _____

tū _____   vōs _____

When would you use a nominative personal pronoun? _____

_____

Lesson Fifty   315

G. DEMONSTRATIVE ADJECTIVE REVIEW

Fill in the demonstrative adjective chants below.

SINGULAR: THIS

Masculine	Feminine	Neuter
hic		

PLURAL: THESE

Masculine	Feminine	Neuter
hī		

SINGULAR: THAT

Masculine	Feminine	Neuter
ille		

PLURAL: THOSE

Masculine	Feminine	Neuter
illī		

H. THIRD CONJUGATION VERB PRACTICE

Translate the third conjugation verbs below from the present, imperfect, future, and perfect tenses. Label the tense.

	TENSE	TRANSLATION
1. adfīgimus		
2. adfīximus		
3. dēligit		
4. dēliget		
5. dēlēgit		
6. reddidistī		
7. reddis		
8. rodent		
9. rodunt		
10. rodēbant		
11. rosērunt		

Lesson Fifty

51 Lesson Fifty-One
Review: Lists 13-16 & Units 7-8

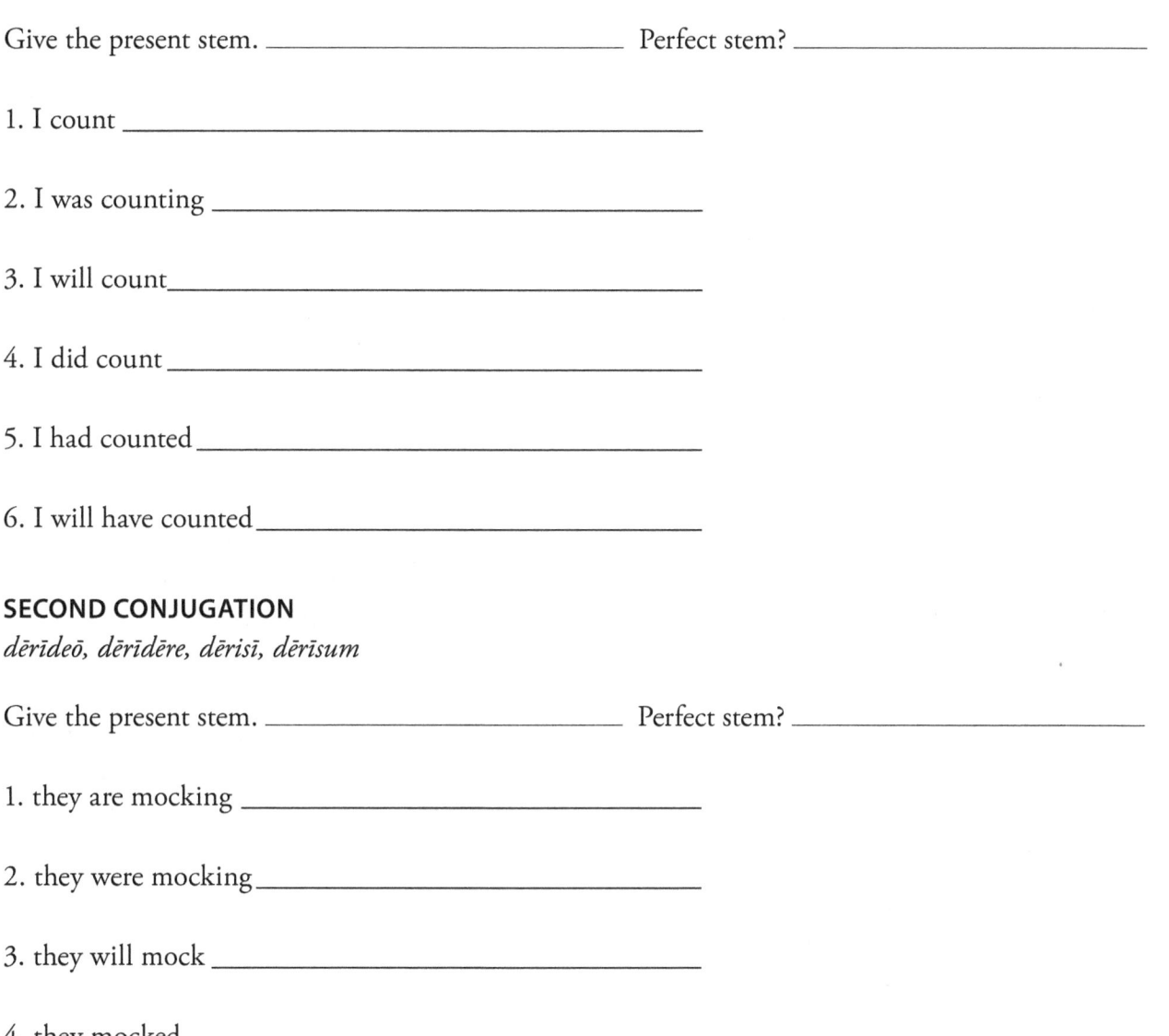

A. VERB TRANSLATION
Translate these verbs into Latin.

FIRST CONJUGATION

numerō, numerāre, numerāvī, numerātum

Give the present stem. _____ Perfect stem? _____

1. I count _____

2. I was counting _____

3. I will count _____

4. I did count _____

5. I had counted _____

6. I will have counted _____

SECOND CONJUGATION

dērīdeō, dērīdēre, dērīsī, dērīsum

Give the present stem. _____ Perfect stem? _____

1. they are mocking _____

2. they were mocking _____

3. they will mock _____

4. they mocked _____

5. they had mocked _____

6. they will have mocked _____

THIRD CONJUGATION
dēdūcō, dēdūcere, dēdūxī, dēductum

Give the present stem. _____ Perfect stem? _____

1. she subtracts _____

2. she was subtracting _____

3. she will subtract _____

4. she did subtract _____

5. she had subtracted _____

6. she will have subtracted _____

B. FORMING COMMANDS
Form commands for the following first and second conjugation verbs. Give both the singular and plural commands. An example is done for you.

	SINGULAR COMMAND	**PLURAL COMMAND**
1. Answer the teacher.	*Respondē magistrum (magistram).*	*Respondēte magistrum.*
2. Sell the eggs.		
3. Milk the cow.		

Form a command for the third conjugation verb below.

4. vanish _____ _____

C. NOUN-ADJECTIVE AGREEMENT WITH NUMBERS

Translate the noun-adjective phrases below using both ordinal and cardinal numbers. Use the nominative case.

1. one young man _____

2. the first young man _____

3. two dresses _____

4. the second dress _____

5. three parties _____

6. the third party _____

7. six eggs _____

8. six girls _____

9. six boys _____

10. the seventh night _____

D. POSSESSIVE ADJECTIVE PRACTICE

Label and translate these sentences containing the possessive adjectives *meus, mea, meum* and *tuus, tua, tuum*. Sentence #3 must be translated into Latin.

1. Virgō tuum lāc portat. _____

2. Vēnditābis meī pullī ōva die. _____

_____

3. Your milkmaid spilled my milk in the dairy. _____

_____

Lesson Fifty-One 321

E. QUI, QUAE, QUOD

Fill in the missing parts of the relative pronoun *qui, quae, quod*.

quī	quae	quod

quī	quae	quae

What does *qui, quae, quod* mean? _____

ACTIVITY PAGES

A List One: Crossword Puzzle

Fill in the Latin translation of the English words below by following the ACROSS and DOWN clues. Match the number of the clue to the numbered boxes going in that direction.

ACROSS
3 tell
5 village
7 study
8 rob
9 I attack
11 I shout
13 I help
16 I frighten
17 Greece
19 I hurry
20 story teller

DOWN
1 warn
2 I care for
4 I laugh
6 Aesop
10 I howl
12 I listen to
14 I swallow
15 story
18 not

Activity Pages 325

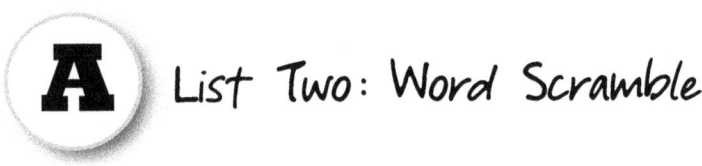 **List Two: Word Scramble**

Unscramble the Latin words below and give their English translations.

                LATIN WORD   TRANSLATION

1. ribel

2. demnamicu

3. sludu

4. tropas

5. pluco

6. smon

7. avinic

8. robola

9. spluu

10. scivinu

11. cousi

12. truemi

13. sivo

14. repu

15. starive

16. mexand

A. List Three: A Race Course

Label the drawing in Latin using words from List 3. Then, for each picture, answer the question *Quid agit?* (What is he/she/it doing?). When you are finished you may color the picture.

For example:
Quid agit arbiter?   <u>*Arbiter metam spectat.*</u>

1. Quid agit Iulius?   _____

2. Quid agit Iulia?   _____

3. Quid agit cuniculus? (use Review List 3 to answer this)   _____

A List Four: Comic Strip

Draw a Latin cartoon using words from List 4 for the captions.

A List Five: Crossword Puzzle

Fill in the Latin translation of the English words below by following the ACROSS and DOWN clues. Match the number of the clue to the numbered boxes going in that direction.

ACROSS
4 autumn
5 dinner
7 in the country
8 female cook
10 eat
11 write
12 many
13 summer
15 acorn
17 grain
19 desk

DOWN
1 lunch
2 pluck
3 letter
6 cheese
8 cook
9 food
14 feast
16 read
18 apple
20 nut

List Six: Word Search

Find the words in the grid. Words can go horizontally, vertically and diagonally in all eight directions.

```
R O R T A L R U K O T F R
L G S K N O R J R C L D U
M P U N X B C R B J K E S
Z U M U I U U A G L T N T
O V C C C S N X V N K S I
T P U I U R N G S U M T C
L S P S T Q O E U U M J U
U M N U B I L T J L B Q S
C I J T V E R H O B A I M
C X H I F C I T E P H L K
O T N R K R M C A N I S Y
X U G A M M S U E L C U N
M N K M A N G U L U S V G
```

angulus
canis
cavum
vinum
dens
feles
insusurro

latro
maritus
mus
nucleus
occulto
poto
rusticus

triticum
ubi
ungula
urbicus
uxor

Activity Pages

 List Seven: A Winter Scene

Draw a picture of a winter weather including a least five words from List 7 Label items in the picture in Latin.

A List Eight:

Write a macaronic story about an ant colony using at least ten words from List 8. Underline the Latin words used.

List Nine: Crossword Puzzle

Fill in the Latin translation of the English words below by following the ACROSS and DOWN clues. Match the number of the clue to the numbered boxes going in that direction.

ACROSS
1 bind
2 throw
6 fierce
7 net
10 drag
11 mercy
13 growl
14 lie
16 hunter
17 flee

DOWN
1 lion
2 beg
3 foot
4 over
5 mane of any animal
8 help
9 set free
12 nibble
13 rope
15 on the ground

A List Ten: Word Search

Find the words in the grid. Words can go horizontally, vertically and diagonally in all eight directions.

```
T L H T F K S I L V A X W D J
F P S M R T L N L N L N N L L
Y E P U T E U V O T I B U D Y
J L P I T K D P R P M N D X M
Y L B C L A H D A L Q R Y U W
F I N I X B R D O C S M D K K
J S H F R M K G K A U N M T V
P M M E W C T G N I P K E N V
S C R N G J V I G Z R M O E C
U D L E L Q M I H C O X S K H
T K K B M A T O T W C T Z D W
S T R T L S R P C A ? P R C D
E F Q Q E U F C Q G C A P I O
A N J V I R K R O M Q T K V P
M L W L V T Z E R A M Q F T T
```

animal	dum	pellis
beneficium	eo	reddo
capio	gratus	silva
caput	iuro	vestigo
corpus	maestus	vestigium
dubito	mare	vita

A List Eleven: Birds

Color the *aves* in the picture and label each one in Latin.

Activity Pages 335

 **List Twelve: Stained Glass Window**

Color the stained glass window, labeling the colors you use. Add your own scene to each pane if desired.

List Thirteen: Crossword Puzzle

Fill in the Latin translation of the English words below by following the ACROSS and DOWN clues. Match the number of the clue to the numbered boxes going in that direction.

ACROSS
1 buy
4 to bear
5 shut out
7 braid
9 market
11 new
13 milk
14 milk pail
15 before
16 dairy maid

DOWN
2 egg
3 sell
4 be able
6 dream
7 hen
8 chicken
10 storeroom
12 cow

List Fourteen: Word Search

Find the words in the grid. Words can go horizontally, vertically and diagonally in all eight directions.

```
S T O Q O E G L U M N N C B E
T U Z C C O N V I V I U M Y V
K V L Z U Q G K A L M G J B A
T R V L Y L M R L M E R E O N
C P G Y E P U Y O V R N W W E
V I R G O B G S C S C T B Y S
S U E C L A C S I G E N T N C
V O Z H B K T M R E G U E L O
O I I T M O Q N G N V C S M A
D T V T L G U G A A S L R I R
N A Y A A M N W L E F P N V N
U T Y T E U B Y L R O U Y F Y
F L K R L L Q U X D C J R Z F
F A O H W Q D Z A E X D N T W
E S T Z X A L C P N P M X Y T
```

adulescens
agricola
bellus
cado
calceus
convivium

effundo
evanesco
gena
mereo
mulgeo
numero

oculus
pecunia
quatio
roseus
saltatio
stola

A List Fifteen: Story Problems

Do the Latin story problems below. Answers must be written in Latin.

1. Iulia tres mures habet. Iulius Iuliae duo mures dat. Quot mures habet Iulia?

   _____

2. Claudia tria spatia currit. Claudius unum spatium currit et Saxum currit duo spatium. Quot spatia currunt liberi et Saxum?

   _____

   _____

3. Saxum decem nuctes habet. Edit unam nuctem. Iuliae duae nuctes dat. Iam *(now)* quot nuctes habet Saxum?

   _____

4. Ludus Iuli et Iuliae decem scholas habet. Omnis *(every)* schola decem mensas habet. Quot mensas habet ludus?

   _____

5. Iulius ad macellum ambulabat. In via decem feles, centum canes, et mille formicas concucurrit *(he met)*. Quot ad macellum ambulabant?

   _____

 **List Sixteen: Word Scramble**

Unscramble the Latin words below and give their English translations.

               LATIN WORD   TRANSLATION

1. xon

2. srean

3. idse

4. oanuqd

5. raavsu

6. snimes

7. upmest

8. tiarn

9. saunn

10. aohr

REFERENCE PAGES

A Note About Chants

Learn all the chants in the order they appear on the page – starting with the far left column and moving down the page; then back to the top of the second column, and so forth. Some of the chants are from Logos Latin 1 and Logos Latin 2, and some are new in Logos Latin 3.

Remember that classical education follows the Trivium and this is a grammar level curriculum. In the grammar stage students memorize and chant many things that they might not understand completely, but as they progress through the Logos Latin series they will build on this knowledge.

 Verb Chants

FIRST CONJUGATION

amō	amāmus
amās	amātis
amat	amant

SECOND CONJUGATION

videō	vidēmus
vidēs	vidētis
videt	vident

THIRD CONJUGATION

dūcō	dūcimus
dūcis	dūcitis
dūcit	dūcunt

FOURTH CONJUGATION

audiō	audīmus
audīs	audītis
audit	audiunt

LINKING VERB (PRESENT TENSE)

sum	sumus
es	estis
est	sunt

POSSUM CHANT

possum	possumus
potes	potestis
potest	possunt

PRESENT TENSE VERB ENDINGS

-ō	-mus
-s	-tis
-t	-nt

FUTURE TENSE VERB ENDINGS

-bō	-bimus
-bis	-bitis
-bit	-bunt

IMPERFECT TENSE VERB ENDINGS

-bam	-bāmus
-bās	-bātis
-bat	-bant

PERFECT TENSE VERB ENDINGS

-ī	-imus
-istī	-istis
-it	-ērunt

FUTURE PERFECT TENSE VERB ENDINGS

-erō	-erimus
-eris	-eritis
-erit	-erint

PLUPERFECT TENSE VERB ENDINGS

-eram	-erāmus
-erās	-erātis
-erat	-erant

Verb Chants (Continued)

PRESENT PASSIVE VERB ENDINGS

-r	-mur
-ris	-minī
-tur	-ntur

FUTURE PASSIVE VERB ENDINGS

-bor	-bimur
-beris	-biminī
-bitur	-buntur

IMPERFECT PASSIVE VERB ENDINGS

-bar	-bamur
-baris	-baminī
-batur	-bantur

Noun Chants

Noun chant endings do not have meanings in the same way that verb endings do. Instead, noun endings can tell what part of speech a word is, such as the subject noun. Like verbs, nouns have different families which are called *declensions*.

FIRST DECLENSION

-a	-ae
-ae	-ārum
-ae	-īs
-am	-ās
-ā	-īs

SECOND DECLENSION

-us	-ī
-ī	-ōrum
-ō	-īs
-um	-ōs
-ō	-īs

SECOND DECLENSION NEUTER

-um	-a
-ī	-ōrum
-ō	-īs
-um	-a
-ō	-īs

THIRD DECLENSION

-x	-ēs
-is	-um
-ī	-ibus
-em	-ēs
-e	-ibus

THIRD DECLENSION - I STEM

-is	-ēs
-is	-ium
-ī	-ibus
-em	-ēs
-e	-ibus

THIRD DECLENSION NEUTER

-x	-a
-is	-um
-ī	-ibus
-x	-a
-e	-ibus

Reference Pages

Noun Chants (Continued)

THIRD DECLENSION NEUTER I-STEM

---x	-ia
-is	-ium
-ī	-ibus
---	-ia
-ī	-ibus

FOURTH DECLENSION

-us	-ūs
-ūs	-uum
-uī	-ibus
-um	-ūs
-ū	-ibus

FOURTH DECLENSION NEUTER

-ū	-ua
-ūs	-uum
-ū	-ibus
-ū	-ua
-ū	-ibus

FIFTH DECLENSION

-ēs	-ēs
-ēī	-ērum
-ēi	-ēbus
-em	-ēs
-ē	-ēbus

Pronoun Chants

DEMONSTRATIVE PRONOUNS (memorize the top two across, not down)

SINGULAR - THIS

hic	haec	hoc
huius	huius	huius
huic	huic	huic
hunc	hanc	hoc
hōc	hāc	hōc

PLURAL - THESE

hī	hae	haec
hōrum	hārum	hōrum
hīs	hīs	hīs
hōs	hās	haec
hīs	hīs	hīs

PERSONAL PRONOUNS

1. SINGULAR - FIRST PERSON (I/ME)

ego
meī
mihi
mē
mē

3. PLURAL - FIRST PERSON (WE)

nōs
nostrum
nōbis
nōs
nōbīs

2. SINGULAR - SECOND PERSON (YOU)

tū
tuī
tibi
tē
tē

4. PLURAL - SECOND PERSON (YOU ALL)

vōs
vestrum
vōbīs
vōs
vōbīs

SINGULAR - THAT

M	F	N
ille	illa	illud
illīus	illīus	illīus
illī	illī	illī
illum	illam	illud
illō	illā	illī

PLURAL - THOSE

M	F	N
illī	illae	illa
illōrum	illārum	illōrum
illīs	illīs	illīs
illōs	illās	illa
illīs	illīs	illīs

SINGULAR - THIS, THAT, HE, SHE, IT

M	F	N
is	ea	id
eius	eius	eius
eī	eī	eī
eum	eam	id
eō	eā	eō

PLURAL - THESE, THOSE, THEY

M	F	N
eī	eae	ea
eorum	eārum	eōrum
eīs	eīs	eīs
eōs	eās	ea
eīs	eīs	eīs

RELATIVE PRONOUN - WHO, WHICH

quī	quae	quod
cuius	cuius	cuius
cui	cui	cui
quem	quam	quod
quo	qua	quo

quī	quae	quae
quorum	quarum	quorum
quibus	quibus	quibus
quos	quas	quae
quibus	quibus	quibus

R Jingles and Nifty Sayings

Five Noun Cases

Nominative	→	NO
Genitive	→	GENTLE
Dative	→	DAD
Accusative	→	ACCUSES
Ablative	→	APPLES

How to Find the Noun Base

Don't try to change the case

   until you find the base.

The genitive case

   is the place to find the base.

And I forgot to mention

   it also shows declension!

LATIN ACTIVE VERB TENSE CHART I

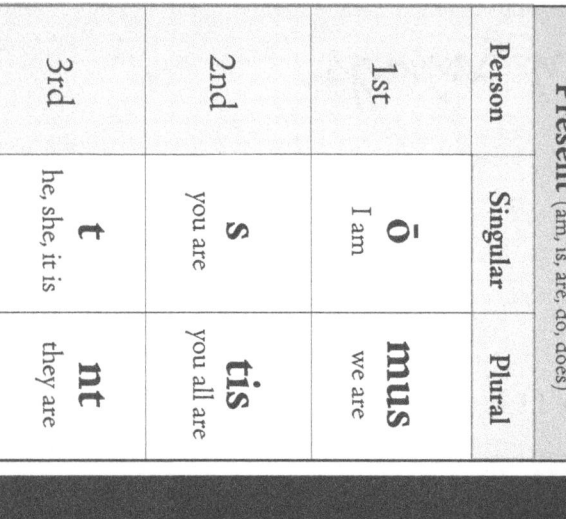

Present (am, is, are, do, does)

Person	Singular	Plural
1st	ō I am	mus we are
2nd	s you are	tis you all are
3rd	t he, she, it is	nt they are

Imperfect (was, were, used to)

Person	Singular	Plural
1st	bam I was	bāmus we were
2nd	bās you were	bātis you all were
3rd	bat he, she, it was	bant they were

Future (will, shall)

Person	Singular	Plural
1st	bō I will	bimus we will
2nd	bis you will	bitis you all will
3rd	bit he, she, it will	bunt they will

Logos Press © 2009

Latin Ending Charts

LATIN NOUN ENDINGS CHART I

CASE KEY   **NOM:** NOMINATIVE   **GEN:** GENITIVE   **DAT:** DATIVE   **ACC:** ACCUSATIVE   **ABL:** ABLATIVE

1st Declension

Case	Singular	Plural
Nom	a	ae
Gen	ae	ārum
Dat	ae	īs
Acc	am	ās
Abl	ā	īs

2nd Declension

Case	Singular	Plural
Nom	us	ī
Gen	ī	ōrum
Dat	ō	īs
Acc	um	ōs
Abl	ō	īs

2nd Declension Neuter

Case	Singular	Plural
Nom	um	a
Gen	ī	ōrum
Dat	ō	īs
Acc	um	a
Abl	ō	īs

3rd Declension

Case	Singular	Plural
Nom	x	ēs
Gen	is	um
Dat	ī	ibus
Acc	em	ēs
Abl	e	ibus

3rd Declension Neuter

Case	Singular	Plural
Nom	x	a
Gen	is	um
Dat	ī	ibus
Acc	x	a
Abl	e	ibus

Latin Ending Charts

LATIN ACTIVE VERB TENSE CHART II

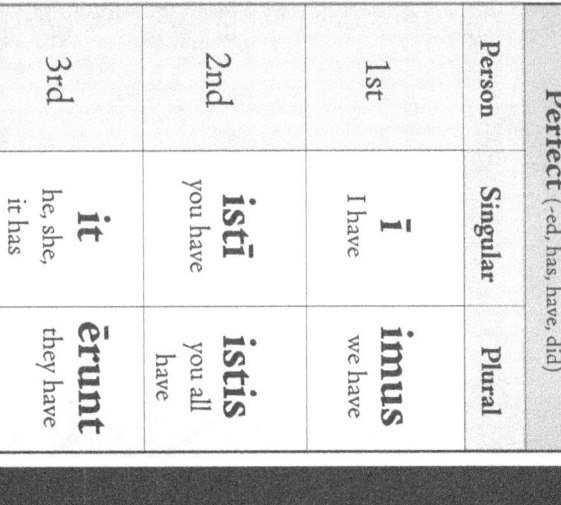

Perfect (-ed, has, have, did)

Person	Singular	Plural
1st	ī — I have	imus — we have
2nd	istī — you have	istis — you all have
3rd	it — he, she, it has	ērunt — they have

Pluperfect (had)

Person	Singular	Plural
1st	eram — I had	erāmus — we had
2nd	erās — you had	erātis — you all had
3rd	erat — he, she, it had	erant — they had

Future Perfect (will have, shall have)

Person	Singular	Plural
1st	erō — I will have	erimus — we will have
2nd	eris — you will have	eritis — you all will have
3rd	erit — he, she, it will have	erint — they will have

Logos Press © 2009

LATIN NOUN ENDINGS CHART II

CASE KEY   **NOM:** NOMINATIVE   **GEN:** GENITIVE   **DAT:** DATIVE   **ACC:** ACCUSATIVE   **ABL:** ABLATIVE

3rd Declension i-Stem

Case	Singular	Plural
Nom	is	ēs
Gen	is	ium
Dat	ī	ibus
Acc	em	ēs
Abl	e	ibus

3rd Declension i-Stem Neuter

Case	Singular	Plural
Nom	x	ia
Gen	is	ium
Dat	ī	ibus
Acc	x	ia
Abl	ī	ibus

4th Declension

Case	Singular	Plural
Nom	us	ūs
Gen	ūs	uum
Dat	uī	ibus
Acc	um	ūs
Abl	ū	ibus

4th Declension Neuter

Case	Singular	Plural
Nom	ū	ua
Gen	ūs	uum
Dat	ū	ibus
Acc	ū	ua
Abl	ū	ibus

5th Declension

Case	Singular	Plural
Nom	ēs	ēs
Gen	ēī	ērum
Dat	ēī	ēbus
Acc	em	ēs
Abl	ē	ēbus

Reference Pages   355

 Memory Work:

Happy Birthday

Tibi diem natalem felicem,
Tibi diem natalem felicem,
Diem natalem felicem carus/cara (name),
Tibi diem natalem felicem!

Genesis 1:1-5

¹ In principio creavit Deus caelum et terram

² terra autem erat inanis et vacua et tenebrae super faciem abyssi et spiritus Dei ferebatur super aquas

³ dixitque Deus fiat lux et facta est lux

⁴ et vidit Deus lucem quod esset bona et divisit lucem ac tenebras

⁵ appellavitque lucem diem et tenebras noctem factumque est vespere et mane dies unus

Genesis 1:1-5 (NKJV)

¹ In the beginning God created the heavens and the earth.

² The earth was without form, and void; and darkness was on the face of the deep. And the Spirit of God was hovering over the face of the waters.

³ Then God said, "Let there be light"; and there was light.

⁴ And God saw the light, that it was good; and God divided the light from the darkness.

⁵ God called the light Day, and the darkness He called Night. So the evening and the morning were the first day.

Memory Work:

Luke 1:46-55, The Magnificat

⁴⁶ et ait Maria magnificat anima mea Dominum

⁴⁷ et exultavit spiritus meus in Deo salutari meo

⁴⁸ quia respexit humilitatem ancillae suae ecce enim ex hoc beatam me dicent omnes generationes

⁴⁹ quia fecit mihi magna qui potens est et sanctum nomen eius

⁵⁰ et misericordia eius in progenies et progenies timentibus eum

⁵¹ fecit potentiam in brachio suo dispersit superbos mente cordis sui

⁵² deposuit potentes de sede et exaltavit humiles

⁵³ esurientes implevit bonis et divites dimisit inanes

⁵⁴ suscepit Israhel puerum suum memorari misericordiae

⁵⁵ sicut locutus est ad patres nostros Abraham et semini eius in saecula

Luke 1:46-55, The Song of Mary

⁴⁶ And Mary said: "My soul magnifies the Lord,

⁴⁷ And my spirit has rejoiced in God my Savior.

⁴⁸ For He has regarded the lowly state of His maidservant; For behold, henceforth all generations will call me blessed.

⁴⁹ For He who is mighty has done great things for me, And holy is His name.

⁵⁰ And His mercy is on those who fear Him From generation to generation.

⁵¹ He has shown strength with His arm; He has scattered the proud in the imagination of their hearts.

⁵² He has put down the mighty from their thrones, And exalted the lowly.

⁵³ He has filled the hungry with good things, And the rich He has sent away empty.

⁵⁴ He has helped His servant Israel, In remembrance of His mercy,

⁵⁵ As He spoke to our fathers, To Abraham and to his seed forever."

 Memory Work:

Canticum David

¹ Dominus pascit me nihil mihi deerit

² in pascuis herbarum adclinavit me super aquas refectionis enutrivit me

³ animam meam refecit duxit me per semitas iustitiae propter nomen suum

⁴ sed et si ambulavero in valle mortis non timebo malum quoniam tu mecum es virga tua et baculus tuus ipsa consolabuntur me

⁵ pones coram me mensam ex adverso hostium meorum inpinguasti oleo caput meum calix meus inebrians

⁶ sed et benignitas et misericordia subsequetur me omnibus diebus vitae meae et habitabo in domo Domini in longitudine dierum

A Psalm of David

¹ The Lord is my shepherd; I shall not want.

² He makes me to lie down in green pastures; He leads me beside the still waters.

³ He restores my soul; He leads me in the paths of righteousness For His name's sake.

⁴ Yea, though I walk through the valley of the shadow of death, I will fear no evil;
For You are with me; Your rod and Your staff, they comfort me.

⁵ You prepare a table before me in the presence of my enemies; You anoint my head with oil;
My cup runs over.

⁶ Surely goodness and mercy shall follow me All the days of my life; And I will dwell[a] in the house of the Lord Forever.

Memory Work:

Pater Noster

¹ Pater noster, quī es in caelīs,

² sanctificētur Nōmen Tuum.

³ adveniat regnum Tuum;

⁴ fiat voluntas Tua

⁵ sīcut in caelō et in terrā.

⁶ Pānem nostrum cotīdiānum dā nōbīs hodiē,

⁷ et dimitte nōbīs dēbita nostra,

⁸ Sīcut et nōs dimittimus dēbitoribus nostrīs,

⁹ et ne nōs inducās in tentātiōnem,

¹⁰ sed līberā nōs a Malō.

¹¹ Āmēn.

The Lord's Prayer

¹ Our Father who art in heaven,

² hallowed be Thy name.

³ Thy kingdom come.

⁴ Thy will be done

⁵ on earth as it is in heaven.

⁶ Give us this day our daily bread,

⁷ and forgive us our trespasses,

⁸ as we forgive those who trespass against us,

⁹ and lead us not into temptation,

¹⁰ but deliver us from evil.

¹¹ Amen.

 Visual Aid: Flower - Verb Stem

(From Lesson Thirteen)

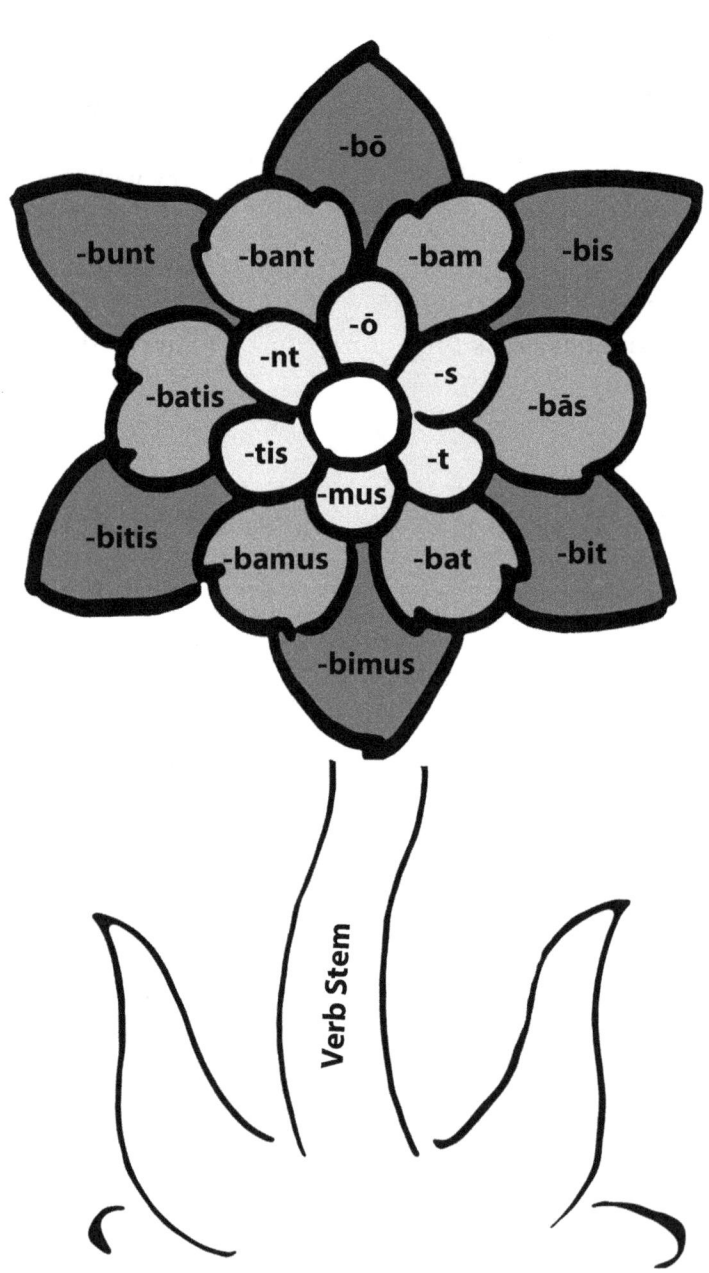

R Visual Aid: Flower - Verb Stem

(From Lesson Forty-Five)

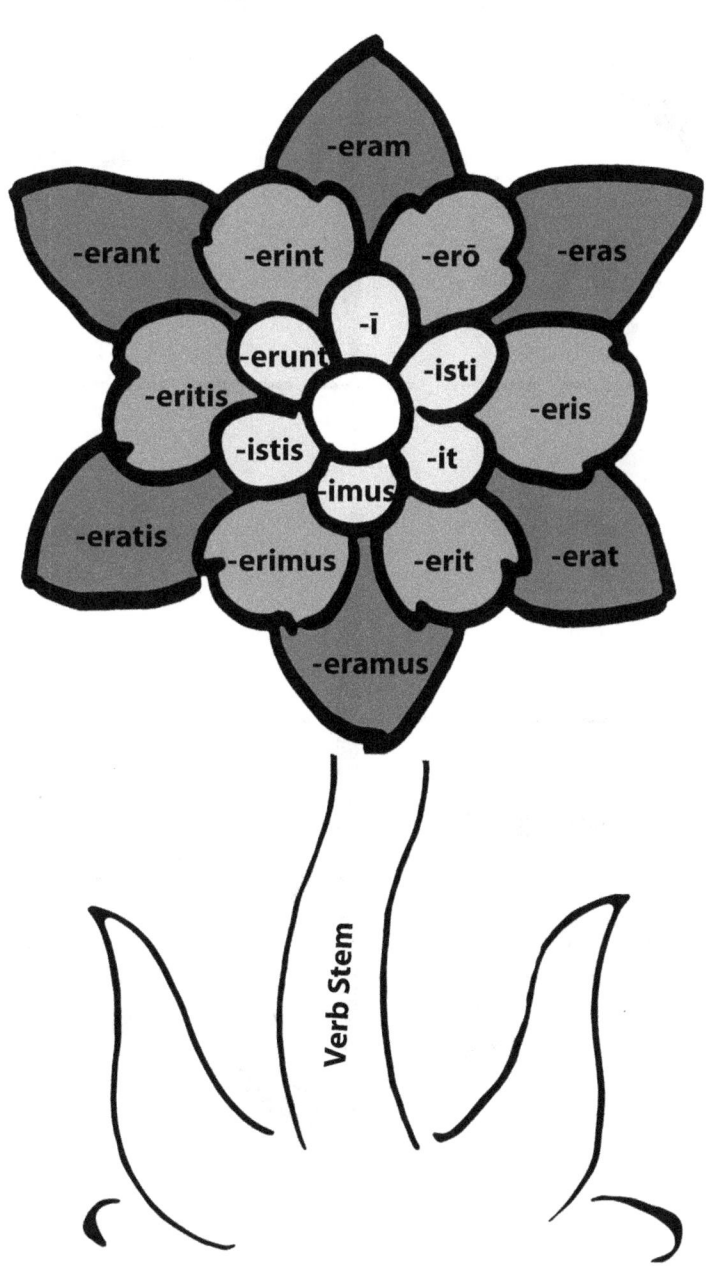

 Visual Aid: "In a Nutshell" - Verb Endings

(From Lesson Seventeen)

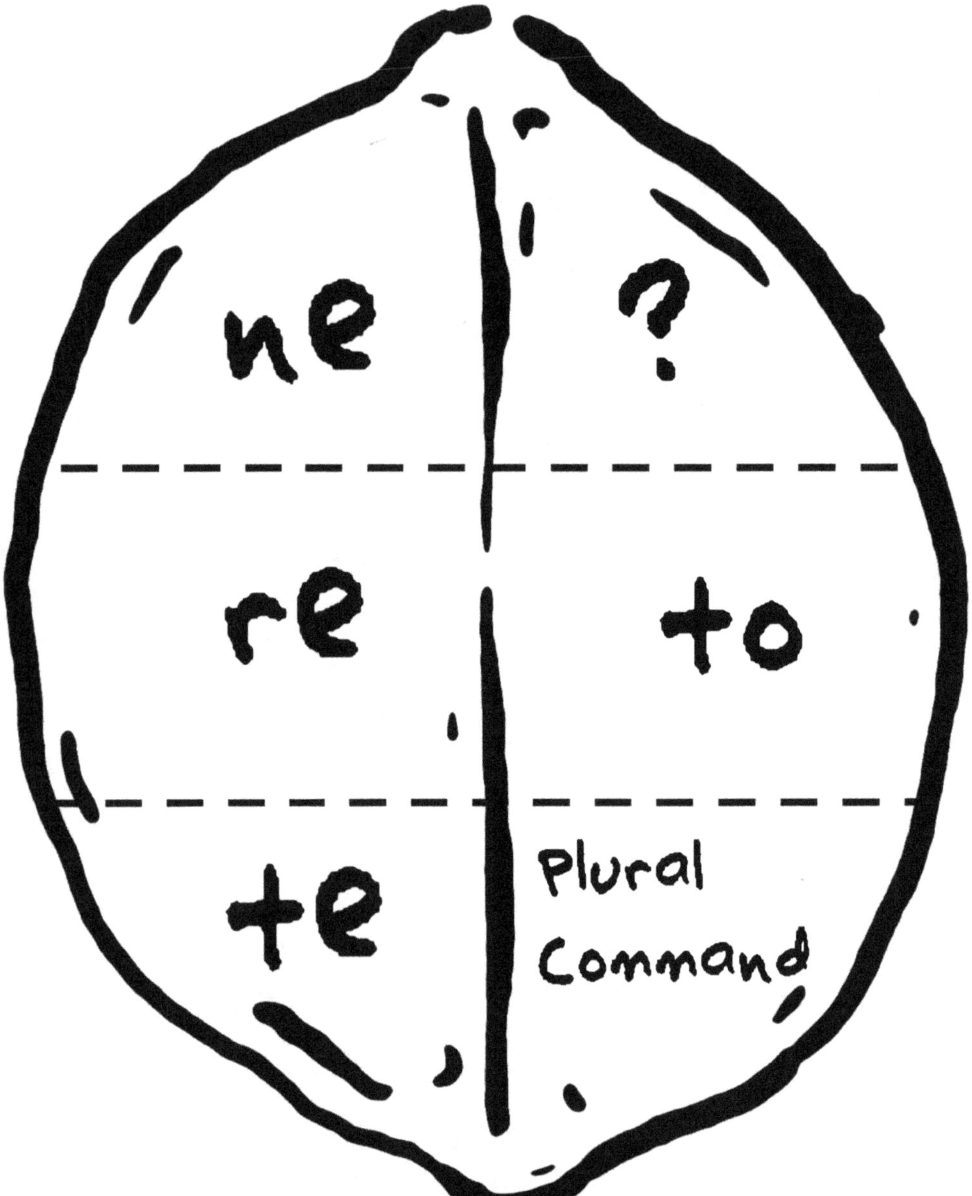

ne	?
re	to
te	Plural Command

Reference Pages

Ordinal Number Comparison Chart

	LATIN	FRENCH	ITALIAN	SPANISH	ROMANIAN
0	nihil	zéro	zero	cero	zero
1	ūnus	un	uno	uno	unu
2	duo	deux	due	dos	doi
3	trēs	trois	tre	tres	trei
4	quattuor	quatre	quattro	cuatro	patru
5	quīnque	cinq	cinque	cinco	cinci
6	sex	six	sei	seis	şase
7	septem	sept	sette	siete	şapte
8	octō	huit	otto	ocho	opt
9	novem	neuf	nove	nueve	nouă
10	decem	dix	dieci	diez	zece
11	ūndecim	onze	undici	once	unsprezece
12	duodēcim	douze	dodici	doce	douăsprezece
100	centum	cent	cento	ciento	o suta
1000	mille	mille	mille	mil	o mie

Glossary: Latin to English

The number in parentheses indicates the list in which the word is introduced. Some words from Logos Latin 1 & 2 appear only in Review Lists. These words are indicated by the abbreviation *Rv.*

A

ā, ab, *prep. w/ abl.*, from, away from (10)
accusō, -āre, -āvī, -ātum, *verb*, accuse (12)
acutus, -a, -um, *adj.*, sharp, pointed (also intelligent)
ad, *prep. w/ acc.*, to, toward (2)
addō, -ere, -didi, -ditium, *verb*, add (15)
adfīgō, -ere, fixī, fixum, *verb*, fasten to, affix (11)
adiūdicō, -are, -āvī, -ātum, *verb*, award (Rv. 16)
administrō, -āre, -āvī, -ātum, *verb*, help, manage (9)
adulēscēns, adulēscentis, *m., noun*, young man (14)
Aesōpus, -ī, *m., noun*, Aesop (1)
aestās, aestātis, *f., noun*, summer (5)
agnus, -ī, *m., noun*, lamb (2)
agricola, -ae, *m., noun*, farmer (14)
albus, -a, -um, *adj.*, white (7)
ambulō, -āre, -āvī, -ātum, *verb*, walk (4)
amīcus, -ī., *m., noun*, friend
amō, -āre, -āvī, -ātum, *verb*, like, love (8)
anas, anatis, *f., noun*, duck (11)
ancilla, ae, *f., noun*, maid
angulus, -i, *m., noun*, corner (6)
animal, -is, *n., noun*, animal (10)
annus, -ī, *m., noun*, year (16)
anser, anseris, *m., noun*, goose (16)
ante, *prep. w/ acc.*, before (13)
apportō, -are, -avi, -ātum, *verb*, bring
aquila, -ae, *f., noun*, eagle (11)
arbiter, arbitrī, *m., noun*, umpire, referee (3)
arbor, arboris, *f., noun*, tree (4)
arithmētica, -ae, *f., noun*, arithmetic (Rv. 15, 16)
augeō, -ēre, -auxī, auctum, *verb*, increase (8)
aureus, -a, -um, *adj.*, golden (12)
auris, auris, *f., noun*, ear (4)
auscultō, -āre, -āvī, -ātum, *verb*, listen to (1)
autumnus, -ī, *m., noun*, autumn (5)
avārus, -a, -um, *adj.*, greedy (16)

avis, avis, *f., noun*, bird (11)

B

bacca, -ae, *f., noun*, berry (Rv. 5)
bellus, -a, -um, *adj.*, pretty (14)
beneficium, -ī, *n., noun*, kindness (10)
brevis somnus, *noun*, a nap (3)

C

cadō, -ere, cecidī, casum, *verb*, fall (14)
caelum, -ī, *n., noun*, sky, heaven(s) (12)
caeruleus, -a, -um, *adj.*, blue (12)
calceus, -ī, *m., noun*, hoe, slipper (14)
canis, canis, *m. or f., noun*, dog (6)
canō, -āre, -āvī, -ātum, *verb*, play (on an instrument) (8)
cantō, -āre, -āvī, -ātum, *verb*, sing (12)
capiō, -ere, cēpī, captum, *verb*, capture (10)
caput, capitis, *n., noun*, head (10)
carpō, -ere, carpsī, carptum, *verb*, pluck (5)
cāseus, -i, *m., noun*, cheese (5)
cavum, -i, *n., noun*, hole (6)
celebrō, -āre, -āvī, -ātum, *verb*, celebrate (8)
cella lactaria, *noun*, dairy (13)
cella, -ae, *f., noun*, storeroom (13)
cēna, -ae, *f., noun*, dinner, meal (5)
centum, *adj.*, a hundred (15)
cibus, -ī, *m.*, noun, food (5)
circum, *prep. w/ acc.*, around (3)
circus, -ī, *m., noun*, an oval race course (3)
cito, *adv.*, swiftly (6)
citus, -a, -um, *adj.*, fast, swift (3)
civis, -is, *m. or f., noun*, citizen
clamō, -āre, -āvī, -ātum, *verb*, shout (Rv. 10)
clāmō, -āre, *verb*, shout (1)
colōnia, -ae, *f., noun*, colony (8)
columba, -ae, *f., noun*, pigeon, dove (11)
conciliō, -āre, -āvi, -ātum, *verb*, win (Rv. 3)
contendo, -tendere, -tendī, -tentum, *verb*, compete (3)
convīvium, -ī, *n., noun*, party (14)

Glossary: Latin to English

convocō, -āre, -āvī, -ātum, *verb, call together (11)*
coqua, -ae, *f., noun, female cook (5)*
coquus, -ī, *m., noun, a cook (5)*
corpus, corporis, *n., noun, body (10)*
culpō, -āre, -āvī, -ātum, *verb,* **blame (2)**
cumulō, -āre, -āvī, -ātum, *verb, heap, pile up (12)*
cunīculus, -ī *m., noun, rabbit (3)*
curo, -are, -avi, -atum, *verb,* **care for (1)**
curriculum, -ī, *n., noun, a race, race course (3)*
curro, currere, cucurrī, cursum, *verb,* **run (3)**
cursor, cursōris, *m., noun, runner (3)*
de, *prep. w/abl., down from, about, concerning (14)*
decem, *adj., ten (15)*
decimus, -a, -um, *adj., tenth (16)*
dedūcō, -ere, -duxī, -ductum, *verb, substract (15)*
defessus, -a, -um, *adj., tired, weary (4)*
deflō, -āre, -āvi, -atum, *verb, blow away (12)*
deligō, -ere, -lēgī, -lectum, *verb, select, choose (11)*
delphīnus, -ī, *m., noun, dolphin (3)*
dens, dentis, *m., noun, tooth (6)*
derideo, -ere, -risi, risum, *verb, mock*
dēvorō, -āre, -āvī, -ātum, *verb, swallow (1)*
diēs natālis, diēī natālis, *m., noun, birthday*
diēs, diēī, *m., noun, day (16)*
discipula, -ae, *f., noun, girl student*
discipulus, -ī, *m., noun, boy student*
diu, *for a long time (8)*
dīvido, -ere, -vīsī, -vīsum, *verb, divide (15)*
do, -āre, dedī, dātum, *verb, give*
domus, ūs, *f., noun, home*
dormitō, -āre, -āvī, -ātum, *verb, dream (13)*
dubitō, -āre, -āvī, -ātum, *verb, doubt, hesitate (10)*
duco, -ere, duxi, ductum, *verb, lead*
dum, *while (10)*
duo, *adj., two (15)*
ē, ex, , *prep. w/abl., out of, from (3)*
edō, -ere, ēdī, ēsum, *verb, eat (5)*
effundō, -ere, -fūdī, -fūsum, *verb, spill, pour out (14)*
emō, -ere, ēmī, emptum, *verb, buy (13)*
eō, -ēre, -rīsi, -rīsum, *verb, mock (10)*
epistula, -ae, *f., noun, letter (5)*
epulae, -ārum, *f., noun, feast (5)*
erat, *verb, was*
errō, -āre, -āvī, -ātum, *verb, wander, err (8)*
est, *verb, he, she, it is*
et, *conj., and*
evānescō, evānescere, evānuī, -------, *verb, vanish, disappear (14)*
excitō, -āre, -āvī, -ātum, *verb, wake (4)*
exclūdō, -ere, -clūsī, -clūsum, *verb, shut out, exclude(for birds - hatch) (13)*
exerceō, -ēre, -uī, -itum, *verb,* **train, exercise (3)**
explōrō, -āre, -āvī, -ātum, *verb, explore (12)*
exspecto, -āre, -āvī, -ātum, *verb,* **wait for, expect (3)**
exspoliō, -āre, *verb, rob (1)*
fābula, -ae, *f., noun, story, fable (1)*
fames, famis, *f., noun, hunger, starvation (8)*
fēles, fēlis, *f., noun, cat (6)*
ferus, -a, -um, *adj., fierce (9)*
fidēs, -ium, *f., noun, lute, lyre, harp (8)*
fīlia, -ae, *f., noun, daughter*
flāvus, -a, -um, *adj., yellow (7)*
flō, -āre, -āvī, -ātum, *verb, blow (7)*
fodicō, -aāre, -āvī, -ātum, *verb, dig*
foedus, -a, -um, *adj., ugly (11)*
folium, -ī, *n., noun, leaf (7)*
formīca, -ae, *f., noun, ant (8)*
fremō, -ere, -uī, -itum, *verb,* **roar, growl (9)**
frūmentum, -i, *n., noun, grain (5)*
fugitō, -āre, -āvī, -ātum, *verb, flee (from) (9)*
fūnis, fūnis, *m., noun, rope (9)*
gallīna, -ae, *f., noun, hen (13)*
gelidus, -a, -um, *adj., cold, icy (7)*
gena, -ae, *f., noun, cheek (14)*
geōgraphia, -ae, *f., noun, geography*
gestō, -āre, -āvī, -ātum, *verb, wear (11)*
glans, glandis, *f., noun, acorn (5)*
globulus, ī, *m., noun, button*
graculus, -ī, *m., noun, jackdaw (11)*
gradus, -ūs, *m., noun, braid (13)*
Graecia, -ae, *f., noun, Greece (1)*

Glossary: Latin to English

grātus, -a, -um, *adj., grateful (10)*
grex, grēgis, *m., noun, flock, herd (2)*
gryllus, -ī, *m., noun, grasshopper (8)*

H
habeō, -ere, -uī, -itum *verb, have, hold*
habitō, -āre, -āvī, -atum, *verb, live in, inhabit*
hiems, hiēmis, *f., noun, winter (7)*
historia, -ae, *f., noun, history*
hōra, -ae, *f., noun, hour (16)*
horreum, -ī, *n., noun, barn*
hortus, -ī, *m., noun garden (7)*
humi, *on the ground (9)*
humus, -ī, *f., noun, ground, earth, soil (7)*
iaceō, -ēre, -uī, *verb, lie (9)*

I
iactō, -āre, -avī, -ātum, *verb, throw (9)*
imperō, -āre, -āvī, -ātum, *verb, order (12)*
implōrō, -āre, -āvi, -ātum, *verb, beg, implore (w/ tears) (9)*
in, *prep. w/abl., in, on (4)*
industrius, -a, -um, *adj., diligent (7)*
inquit, *verb,* **he, she, it said**
insusurrō, -āre, -āvī, -ātum, *verb whisper (6)*
intellegō, -ere, -lexī, -lectum, *verb, realize, understand (12)*
inter, *prep. w/acc., between, among (11)*
intra, *prep. w/abl., inside (16)*
invītō, -āre, -āvī, -ātum, *verb, invite*
iocus, -ī, *m., noun, joke (2)*
irātus, -a, -um, *adj., angry*
iterum, *adv., again (2)*
iuba, -ae, *f., noun, mane of any animal (9)*
Iuppiter, Iovis, *m., noun, Jupiter (11)*
iūrō, -āre, -āvī, -ātum, *verb, swear, take an oath (10)*
iuvo, -are, -iuvi, iutum, *verb, help (1)*
labor, laboris, *f., noun, work, toil (7)*

L
laborō, -āre, -āvī, -ātum, *verb, work (2)*
lac, lactis, *n., noun, milk (13)*
lactaria, -ae, *f., noun, dairy maid (13)*
latrō, -āre, -āvi, -atum, *verb, bark (6)*
laudō, -āre, -āvī, -ātum, *verb, praise (8)*
lavō, -āre, -āvī, -ātum, *verb, wash (11)*
legō, -ere, lēgī, lectum, *verb, read, gather, collect (5, 7)*
leo, leōnis, *m., noun, lion (9)*
lepus, leporis, *m., noun, hare (4)*
liber, libri, *m., noun, book (2)*
līberī, līberōrum, *m., noun, children*
liberō, -āre, -āvi, -ātum, *verb, free, set free (9)*
ligō, -āre, -āvi, -ātum, *verb, bind (9)*
līmo, -are, -avi, -atum, *verb, polish*
longus, -a, -um, *adj., long (4)*
lūdo, lūdere, lūsī, lūsum, *verb,* **play (3)**
lūdus, -ī, *m., noun, school (2)*
lupus, -ī, *m., noun, wolf (2)*

M
macellum, -ī, *n., noun, market (13)*
maestus, -a, -um, *adj., sad (10)*
magister, magistrī, *m., noun, male teacher*
magistra, -ae, *f., noun, female teacher*
magnificus, -a, -um, *adj., magnificent (11)*
magnus, -a, -um, *adj., large*
mālum, -i, *n., noun, apple (5)*
malus, -a, -um, *adj., wicked, bad, evil*
mare, -is, *n., noun, sea (10)*
maritus, -i, *m., noun, husband (6)*
mendacium, -ī, *n., noun, a lie, falsehood (2)*
mendax, mendācis, *m., noun, a liar (2)*
mensa secunda, -ae, *f., noun, dessert (5)*
mensa, -ae, *f., noun, desk, table*
mensis, -is, *m., noun, month (16)*
mereō, -ere, -uī, -itum, *verb, earn, deserve (14)*
messis, -is, *f., noun, harvest (7)*
mēta, -ae, *f., noun, goal (3)*
mīca, -ae, *f., noun, crumb (8)*
mille, *adj., a thousand (15)*
misericordia, -ae, *f., noun, pity, mercy (9)*
moneō, -ēre, -uī, -itum, *verb, warn (1)*
mons, montis, *m., noun, mountain (2)*
monstrō, -āre, -āvī, -ātum, *verb, show, point out*
mulctra, -ae, *f., noun, milk pail (13)*
mulgeō, mulgēre, mulsī, -------, *verb, milk (14)*
multiplicō, -āre, -āvī, -ātum, *verb, multiply (15)*
multus, -a, -um, *adj., much, many (5)*
mundus, -ī, *m., noun, world (12)*
mūs, mūris, *m. or f., noun, mouse (6)*

Glossary: Latin to English

mūs, mūris, *m., noun,* mouse
mūsica, -ae, *f., noun,* music
narrātor, narratōris, *m., noun,* story teller (1)
narrō, -āre, *verb,* tell, say (1)
nīdus, -ī, *m., noun,* nest (12)
niger, -gra, -grum, *adj.,* black (12)
niveus, -a, -um, *adj.,* snowy (7)
nix, nīvis, *f., noun,* snow (7)
nōn, *adv.,* not (1)
nōnus, -a, -um, *adj.,* ninth (16)
novem, *adj.,* nine (15)
novus, -a, -um, *adj.,* new (13)
nox, noctis, *f., noun,* night (16)
nucleus, -i, *m., noun,* kernel (6)
numerō, -āre, -āvī, -ātum, *verb,* count (14)
numerus, -ī, *m., noun,* number (15)
nuntiō, -āre, -āvī, -ātum, *verb,* announce (12)
nunc, *adv,* now
nux, nucis, *f., noun,* nut (5)
obsecrō, -āre, -āvī, -ātum, *verb,* beg, implore
occultō, -āre, -āvī, -ātum, *verb,* hide (6)
octāvus, -a, -um, *adj.,* eighth (16)
octō, *adj.,* eight (15)
oculus, -ī, *m., noun,* eye (14)
oppugnō, -āre, -āvī, -ātum, *verb,* attack (1)
ova parere, *verb,* to lay eggs (13)
ovis, ovis, *f., noun,* sheep (2)
ovum, -ī, *n., noun,* egg
panis, panis, *m., noun,* bread (7)
parens, parentis, *m. or f., noun,* parent
pariō, -ere, peperī, partum, *verb,* bear, bring forth (13)
parō, -āre, -āvī, -ātum, *verb,* prepare (8)
parvus, -a, -um, *adj.,* little, small
pastor, pastōris, *m., noun,* shepherd (2)
pāvo, pavōnis, *m., noun,* peacock (11)
pecūnia, -ae, *f., noun,* money (14)
pellis, -is, *f., noun,* hide, skin (10)
per, *prep. w/acc.,* through (8)
pēs, pedis, *m., noun,* foot, paw (9)
piger, -gra, -grum, *adj.,* lazy (7)
pinna, -ae, *f., noun,* feather (11)
plaga, -ae, *f., noun,* net (for hunting) (9)
pōmum, ī, *n., noun,* fruit
porto, -āre, -avī, -ātum, *verb,* carry
possum, posse, potui, ------, *verb,* be able
potō, -āre, -āvī, -ātum, *verb,* drink (6)
praedium, -ī, *n., noun,* farm
praemium, -ī, *n., noun,* prize
prandium, -ī, *n., noun,* lunch (5)
prīmus, -a, -um, *adj.,* **first** (16)
prope, *prep w/acc.,* near (12)
properō, -āre, -āvi, -ātum, *verb,* hurry, hasten (1)
puer, -ī, *m., noun,* boy, child (2)
pulcher, -chra, -chrum, *adj.,* beautiful, handsome (11)
pullus, -ī, *m., noun,* chicken or chick (13)
quando (interrogative) when? (16)
quārtus, -a, -um, *adj.,* fourth (16)
quatiō, quatere, quassī, quassum, *verb,* shake (14)
quattuor, *adj.,* four (15)
quid, what
quinque, *adj.,* five (15)
quīntus, -a, -um, *adj.,* fifth (16)
quis, who
quod, *conj.,* because
quoque, *adv.,* also (12)
quot (indeclinable adj.), how many? (15)
reddō, -ere, -didi, -ditum, *verb,* repay (10)
rēgīna, -ae, *f., noun,* queen (8)
reservō, -āre, -āvī, -ātum, *verb,* save, lay up, reserve (8)
respondeō, -ēre, respondī, responsum, *verb,* respond, answer (15)
responsum, -ī, *n., noun,* an answer, response (15)
rēx, rēgis, *m., noun,* king (Rv. 10)
rīdeō, -ēre, rīsī, rīsum, *verb,* **laugh, smile** (Rv. 10)
rīdeō, -ēre, *verb,* laugh, smile (1)
rīpa, -ae, *f., noun,* bank (of river, stream) (12)
rīvus, -ī, *m., noun,* stream (11)
rōdō, -ere, rōsī, rōsum, *verb,* nibble, gnaw (9)
rogō, -āre, -āvi, -ātum, *verb,* ask

Glossary: Latin to English

roseus, -a, -um, *adj., rosy, pink* (14)
ruber, rubra, rubrum, *adj., red* (12)
rurī, in the country (5)
rūs, rūris, *n., noun, the country* (2)
rusticus, -a, -um, *adj., belonging to the country* (6)

S

saltātio, -ōnis, *f., noun, a dance* (14)
saltō, -āre, -āvī, -ātum, *verb, dance* (8)
sapientia, -ae, *f., noun, wisdom* (8)
schola, -ae, *f., noun, classroom*
scrībo, -ere, scripsī, scriptum, *verb, write* (5)
scrībō, -ere, scripsi, scriptum, *verb, write*
secundus, -a, -um, *adj., second* (16)
sed, *conj., but* (7)
sedeō, -ēre, sedī, sessum, *verb, sit*
septem, *adj.,* **seven** (15)
septimus, -a, -um, *adj., seventh* (16)
sex, *adj., six* (15)
sextus, -a, -um, *adj., sixth* (16)
sī placet, please (10)
silva, -ae, *f., noun, forest* (10)
somnus, -ī, *m., noun,* **sleep** (3)
somous, -ī, *m., noun, sleep*
spatium, -ī, *n., noun, lap (in a race)* (3)
spectō, -āre, -āvī, -atum, *verb, look at, watch*
stō, -āre, stetī, -ātum, *verb, stand*
stola, -ae, *f., noun, dress* (14)
studeō, -ēre, -uī, --------, *verb, study* (1)
stultus, -a, -um, *adj., foolish* (4)
stultus, -a, -um, *adj., foolish*
sub, *prep. w/abl., under* (4)
super, *prep. w/acc., over, above* (9)
superbe, *adv.,* **proudly**
superbus, -a, -um, *adj., proud* (4)

T

tardō, -āre, -āvi, -ātum, *verb, slow down, delay* (4)
tardus, -a, -um, *adj., slow* (3)
tempestās, -ātis, *f., noun, weather, storm* (7)
tempus, temporis, *n., noun, time* (16)
terra, -ae, *f., noun, ground, earth, land* (Rv. 12)
terreō, -ēre, -uī, -itum, *verb, frighten* (1)
tertius, -a, -um, *adj., third* (16)
testa, -ae, *f., noun, shell* (4)
testūdo, testūdinis, *f., noun, turtle, tortoise* (4)
trahō, -ere, traxī, tractum, *verb, drag* (9)
trans, *prep. w/acc., across* (8)
trēs, *adj., three* (15)
triticum, -i, *n., noun, wheat* (6)
tum, *adv.,* **then** (12)
turgeō, -ēre, tursī,---------, *verb, well up* (4)

U

ubi, *adv., where* (6)
ululō, -āre, *verb, howl* (1)
ungula, -ae, *f., noun, claw* (6)
ūnus, *adj., one* (15)
urbicus, -a, -um, *adj., belonging to the city* (6)
ūtor, *verb, use* (4)
uxor, uxoris, *f., noun, wife* (6)

V

vacca, -ae, *f., noun, cow* (13)
vānus, -a, -um, *adj.,* **vain** (11)
vellō, -ere, vellī, vulsum, *verb, pluck* (11)
vēnātor, -ōris, *m., noun, hunter* (9)
venditō, -āre, āvī, -ātum, *verb, sell* (13)
ventōsus, -a, -um, *adj., windy* (7)
ventus, -ī, *m., noun, wind* (7)
vēritās, vēritātis, *f., noun, truth* (2)
vestīgium, -ī, *n., noun, footprint, track* (10)
vestīgō, -āre, -āvī, -ātum, *verb, track* (10)
vestis, vestis *m., noun, clothing, garment*
via, viae, *f., noun, road, way* (4)
vīcīna, -ae, *f., noun, female neighbor* (2)
vīcīnus, -ī, *m., noun, male neighbor* (2)
victor, victōris, *m., noun, winner* (4)
vīcus, -i, *m., noun, village* (1)
videō, -ēre, vīdī, visum, *verb,* see
vīnum, -i, *n., noun, wine* (6)
virgo, virginis, *f., noun, young woman, maiden* (14)
viridis, -e, *adj., green* (12)
visitō, -āre, -āvi, ātum, *verb, visit*
vīta, -ae, *f., noun, life* (10)
vocō, -āre, -āvī, -ātum, *verb, call*
volō, -āre, -āvi, -ātum, *verb,* fly (4)
vulpēs, vulpis, *f., noun,* fox (4)

Glossary: English to Latin

The number in parentheses indicates the list in which the word is introduced. Some words from Logos Latin 1 and 2 appear only in Review Lists. These words are indicated by the abbreviation *Rv.*.

A

(to) be able, *verb,* **possum, posse, potui, --------** **(13)**
above, *prep. w/acc.,* super (9)
(to) accuse, *verb,* accusō, -āre, -āvī, -ātum (12)
acorn, *noun,* glans, glandis, f. (5)
across, *prep. w/acc.,* trans (8)
ad, *prep. w/ abl.,* to, toward, at
(to) add, *verb,* addō, -ere, -didi, -ditium (15)
Aesop, *noun,* Aesōpus, -ī, m. (1)
(to) affix, *verb,* adfīgō, -ere, fīxī, fīxum (11)
again, *adv.,* iterum (2)
also, *adv.,* quoque (12)
among, *prep. w/acc.* inter (11)
and, *conj.,* et
angry, *adj.,* irātus, -a, -um
animal, *noun,* animal, -is, n. (10)
(to) announce, *verb,* nuntiō, -āre, -āvī, -ātum (12)
(to) answer, *verb,* respondeō, -ēre, respōnsī, respōnsum (15)
ant, *noun,* formīca, -ae, f. (8)
apple, *noun,* mālum, -i, n. (5)
arithmetic, *noun,* arithmētica, -ae, f.
around, *prep. w/acc.,* circum **(3)**
(to) ask, *verb,* rogō, -āre, -āvi, -ātum
(to) attack, *verb,* oppugnō, -āre, -āvī, -ātum (1)
autumn, *noun,* autumnus, -i, m. (5)
(to) award, *verb,* adiūdicō, -are, -āvī, -ātum

B

bad, *adj.,* malus, -a, -um
bank (of river), *noun,* rīpa, -ae, f. (12)
(to) bark, *verb,* latrō, -āre, -āvi, -atum (6)
barn, *noun,* horreum, -ī, n. (Rv. 14)
(to) bear, *verb,* pariō, -ere, peperī, partum (13)
beautiful, *adj.,* pulcher, -chra, -chrum (11)
because, *conj.,* quod (Rv. 12)
before, *prep. w/acc.,* ante **(13)**
(to) beg, *verb,* implōrō, -āre, -āvī, -ātum (9)
belonging to the city, *adj.,* urbicus, -a, -um (6)
belonging to the country, *adj.,* rusticus, -a, -um (6)
berry, *noun,* bacca, -ae, f. (Rv. 5)
between, *prep. w/acc.* inter (11)
(to) bind, *verb,* ligō, -āre, -avi, -ātum (9)
bird, *noun,* avis, avis, f. (11)
birthday, *noun,* diēs natālis, diēī natālis, m. (Rv. 16)
black, *adj.,* niger, -gra, -grum (12)
(to) blame, *verb,* culpō, -āre, -āvī, -ātum (2)
(to) blow away, *verb,* deflō, -āre, -avi, -ātum (12)
(to) blow, *verb,* flō, -āre, -āvī, -ātum (7)
blue, *adj.,* caeruleus, -a, -um (12)
body, *noun,* corpus, corporis, n. (10)
book, *noun,* liber, libri, m. (2)
boy, *noun,* **puer, -ī,** m.(2)
braid, *noun,* gradus, -ūs, m. (13)
bread, *noun,* panis, panis, m. (7)
(to) bring forth, *verb,* pariō, -ere, peperī, partum (13)
(to) bring, *verb,* apportō, -are, -avi, -ātum
but, *conj.,* sed (7)
button, *noun,* globulus, ī, m.
(to) buy, *verb,* emō, -ere, ēmī, emptum (13)

C

(to) call together, *verb,* convocō, -āre, -āvī, -ātum (11)
(to) call, *verb,* vocō, -āre, -āvī, -ātum
(to) capture, *verb,* capiō, -ere, cēpī, captum **(10)**
(to) care for, *verb,* curo, -are, -avi, -atum **(1)**
carry, *verb,* porto, -āre, -avi, -ātum
cat, *noun,* fēles, fēlis, f. (6)
(to) celebrate, *verb,* celebrō, -āre, -āvī, -ātum (8)
cheek, *noun,* gena, -ae, f. (14)
cheese, *noun,* cāseus, -i, m. (5)
chicken, *noun,* pullus, -ī, m. (13)
children, *noun,* līberī, līberōrum, m.
(to) choose, *verb,* deligō, -ere, -lēgī, -lectum **(11)**

Glossary: English to Latin

citizen, *noun,* civis, -is, m. or f.
classroom, *noun,* schola, -ae, f.
claw, *noun,* ungula, -ae, f. (Rv. 10)
claw, *noun,* ungula, -ae, f. (6)
clothing, *noun,* vestis, vestis m.
cold, *adj.,* gelidus, -a, -um (7)
(to) collect, *verb,* legō, -ere, lēgī, lectum (7)
colony, *noun,* colōnia, -ae, f. (8)
(to) compete, *verb,* contendo, -tendere, -tendī, -tentum (3)
(a) cook (female), *noun,* coqua, -ae, f. (5)
(a) cook, *noun,* coquus, -ī, m. (5)
corner, *noun,* angulus, -i, m. (6)
(to) count, *verb,* numerō, -āre, -āvī, -ātum (14)
(a) country, *noun,* rūs, rūris, n. (2)
cow, *noun,* vacca, -ae, f. (13)
crumb, *noun,* mīca, -ae, f. (8)

D

dairy maid, *noun,* lactaria, -ae, f. (13)
(a) dance, *noun,* saltātio, -ōnis, f. (14)
(to) dance, *verb,* **saltō, -āre, -āvī, -ātum (8)**
daughter, *noun,* fīlia, -ae, f.
day, *noun,* diēs, diēī, m. (16)
(to) delay, *verb,* tardō, -āre, -āvī, -ātum (4)
dessert, *noun,* mensa secunda, -ae, f. (5)
(to) dig, *verb,* fodicō, -aāre, -āvī, -ātum
diligent, *adj.,* industrius, -a, -um (7)
dinner, *noun,* cēna, -ae, f. (5)
(to) divide, *verb,* dīvido, -ere, -vīsī, -vīsum (15)
dog, *noun,* canis, canis, m. or f. (6)
dolphin, *noun,* delphīnus, -ī, m. (3)
(to) doubt, *verb,* dubitō, -āre, -āvī, -ātum (10)
dove, *noun,* columba, -ae, f. (11)
down from, *prep. w/abl.,* de (14)
(to) drag, *verb,* trahō, -ere, traxī, tractum **(9)**
(to) dream, *verb,* dormitō, -āre, -āvī, -ātum (13)
dress, *noun,* stola, -ae, f. (14)
drink, *verb,* potō, -āre, -āvī, -atum (6)
duck, *noun,* anas, anatis, f. (11)

E

eagle, *noun,* aquila, -ae, f. (11)
ear, *noun,* auris, auris, f. (4)
earn, *verb,* mereō, -ere, -uī, -itum (14)
earth, *noun,* humus, -ī, f. (7)
(to) eat, *verb,* edō, -ere, ēdī, ēsum (5)
egg, *noun,* ovum, -ī, n. (13)
eight, *adj.,* octō (15)
eighth, *adj.,* octāvus, -a, -um (16)
(to) err, *verb,* errō, -āre, -āvī, -ātum (8)
evil, *adj.,* malus, -a, -um (Rv. 4)
(to) exclude, *verb,* exclūdō, -ere, -clūsī, -clūsum (13)
(to) exercise, *verb,* exerceō, -ēre, -uī, -itum **(3)**
(to) expect, *verb,* exspecto, -āre, -āvī, -ātum (3)
(to) explore, *verb,* explōrō, -āre, -āvī, -ātum (12)
eye, *noun,* oculus, -ī, m. (14)

F

fable, *noun,* fābula, -ae, f. (1)
(to) fall, *verb,* cadō, -ere, cecidī, casum (14)
farm, *noun,* praedium, -ī, n.
farmer, *noun,* agricola, -ae, m. (14)
fast, *adj.,* citus, -a, -um (3)
(to) fasten to, *verb,* adfigō, -ere, fixī, fixum (11)
feast, *noun,* epulae, -ārum, f. (5)
feather, *noun,* pinna, -ae, f. (11)
fierce, *adj.,* ferus, -a, -um (9)
first, *adj.,* prīmus, -a, -um (16)
fifth, *adj.,* quīntus, -a, -um (16)
five, *adj.,* quinque (15)
(to) flee, *verb,* fugitō, -āre, -āvī, -ātum (9)
flock, *noun,* **grex, grēgis,** m. (2)
(to) fly, *verb,* volō, -āre, -avi, -ātum (4)
food, *noun,* cibus, -ī, m. (5)
foolish, *adj.,* stultus, -a, -um **(4)**
foot, *noun,* pēs, pedis, m. (9)
footprint, *noun,* vestīgium, -ī, n. (10)
for a long time, *phrase,* diu (8)
forest, *noun,* silva, -ae, f. (10)
four, *adj.,* quattuor (15)
fourth, *adj.,* quārtus, -a, -um (16)
fox, *noun,* vulpēs, vulpis, f. (4)
(to) free, *verb,* liberō, -āre, -āvī, -ātum (9)
friend, *noun,* amīcus, -ī., m.
(to) frighten, *verb,* terreō, -ēre, -uī, -itum
(to) frighten, *verb,* **terrō, -ēre (1)**
from, *prep. w/abl.,* ā, ab (10)
from, *prep. w/abl.,* ē, ex (3)

Glossary: English to Latin

G

fruit, *noun, pōmum, -ī, n.*
garden, *noun, hortus, -ī, m. (7)*
(to) gather, *verb, legō, -ere, lēgī, lectum*
geography, *noun, geōgraphia, -ae, f.*
(to) give, *verb, do, -āre, -dēdī, -ātum*
goal, *noun, mēta, -ae, f. (3)*
golden, *adj., aureus, -a, -um (12)*
goose, *noun, anser, anseris, m. (16)*
Graecia, *noun, Graecia, -ae, f.* **(1)**
grain, *noun, frūmentum, -i, n. (5)*
grasshopper, *noun, gryllus, -ī, m. (8)*
grateful, *adj., grātus, -a, -um (10)*
greedy, *adj., avārus, -a, -um (16)*
green, *adj., viridis, -e (12)*
(to) growl, *verb, fremō, -ere, -uī, -itum* **(9)**

H

handsome, *adj., pulcher, -chra, -chrum (11)*
hare, *noun,* **lepus, leporis,** *m. (4)*
harp, *noun, fidēs, -ium, f. (8)*
harvest, *noun, messis, -is, f. (7)*
(to) hatch, shut out, *excludō, -ere, -clūsī, -clūsum*
(to) have, *verb, habeo, -ere, -ui, -itum*
head, *noun, caput, capitis, n. (10)*
(to) heap, *verb, cumulō, -āre, -āvī, -ātum (12)*
heaven(s), *noun, caelum, -ī, n. (12)*
(to) help, *verb, administrō, -āre, -āvī, -ātum (9)*
(to) help, *verb, iuvō, -āre (1)*
hen, *noun, gallīna, -ae, f. (13)*
herd, *noun,* **grex, grēgis,** *m. (2)*
(to) hesitate, *verb, dubitō, -āre, -āvī, -ātum (10)*
hide (on an animal), *noun, pellis, -is, f. (10)*
(to) hide, *verb, occultō, -āre, -āvī, -ātum (6)*
history, *noun, historia, -ae, f. (Rv. 16)*
(to) hold, *verb, habeō, -ēre, -uī, -itum (Rv. 14)*
hole, *noun, cavum, -i, n. (6)*
home, *noun, domus, ūs, f. (Rv. 4)*
hour, *noun, hōra, -ae, f. (16)*
how many, *(indeclinable adj.) quot (15)*
(to) howl, *verb, ululō, -āre (1)*
(a) hundred, *adj., centum (15)*
hunger, *noun, fames, famis, f. (8)*
hunter, *noun, vēnātor, -ōris, m. (9)*
(to) hurry, *verb, properō, -āre, -āvi, -ātum (1)*

I

husband, *noun, maritus, -i, m. (6)*
(to) implore, *verb, implōrō, -āre, -āvi, -ātum (9)*
in the country, *phrase, rurī (5)*
in, *prep. w/abl., in (4)*
(to) increase, *verb, augeō, -ēre, -auxī, auctum (8)*
(to) inhabit, *verb, habitō, -āre*
inside, *prep. w/abl., intra (16)*
(to) invite, *verb, invītō, -āre, -āvī, -ātum (Rv. 5)*

J

(he/she/it) is, *verb, est (Rv. 4)*
jackdaw, *noun, graculus, -ī, m. (11)*
joke, *noun, iocus, -ī, m. (2)*

K

Jupiter, *noun, Iuppiter, Iovis, m. (11)*
kernel, *noun, nucleus, -i, m. (6)*
kindness, *noun, beneficium, -ī, n. (10)*
king, *noun, rēx, rēgis, m. (Rv. 10)*

L

lamb, *noun, agnus, -ī, m. (2)*
(a) lap, *noun, spatium, -ī, n. (3)*
large, *adj., magnus, -a, -um (Rv. 9)*
(to) laugh, *verb, rīdeō, -ēre, rīsī, rīsum* **(1)**
(to) lay eggs, *verb, ova parere (13)*
lazy, *adj., piger, -gra, -grum (7)*
lead, *verb, -duco, -ere, duxi, ductum*
leaf, *noun, folium, -ī, n. (7)*
letter, *noun, epistula, -ae, f. (5)*
liar, *noun, mendax, mendācis, m.(2)*
(a) lie, *noun, mendacium, -ī, n. (2)*
(to) lie, *verb, iaceō, -ēre, -uī (9)*
life, *noun, vīta, -ae, f. (10)*
lion, *noun, leo, leōnis, m. (9)*
(to) listen to, *verb, auscultō, -āre, -āvī, -ātum (1)*
little, *adj., parvus, -a, -um* **(Rv. 9)**
long, *adj., longus, -a, -um (4)*
(to) love, *verb, amō, -āre, -āvī, -ātum (8)*
lunch, *noun, prandium, -ī, n. (5)*
lute, *noun, fidēs, -ium, f. (8)*
lyre, *noun, fidēs, -ium, f. (8)*

M

market, *noun, macellum, -ī, n. (13)*
female teacher, *noun, magistra, -ae, f.*
magnificent, *adj., magnificus, -a, -um (11)*
maid, *noun, ancilla, ae, f.*
(to) manage, *verb, administrō, -āre, -āvī, -ātum (9)*

Glossary: English to Latin

mane (of an animal), noun, iuba, -ae, f. (9)
many, adj., multus, -a, -um (5)
meal, noun, cēna, -ae, f. (5)
mercy, noun, misericordia, -ae, f. (9)
milk pail, noun, mulctra, -ae, f. (13)
milk, noun, lac, lactis, n (13)
(to) milk, verb, mulgeō, mulgēre, mulsī, ------- (14)
(to) mock, verb, eō, -ēre, -rīsi, -rīsum (10)
money, noun, pecūnia, -ae, f. (14)
month, noun, mensis, -is, m. (16)
mountain, noun, mons, montis, m.(2)
mouse, noun, mūs, mūris, m. or f. (6)
much, adj., multus, -a, -um (5)
(to) multiply, verb, multiplicō, -āre, -āvī, -ātum (15)
music, noun, mūsica, -ae, f. (Rv. 16)

N

(a) nap, noun, brevis somnus (3)
near, prep w/acc., prope (12)
neighbor (female), noun, vīcīna, -ae, f. (2)
neighbor (male), noun, vīcīnus, -ī, m. (2)
nest, noun, nīdus, -ī, m. (12)
net, noun, plaga, -ae, f. (9)
new, adj., novus, -a, -um (13)
nibble, verb, rōdō, -ere, rōsī, rōsum (9)
night, noun, nox, noctis, f. (16)
nine, adj., novem (15)
ninth, adj., nōnus, -a, -um (16)
not, adv., nōn, (1)
now, adv., nunc

O

number, noun, numerus, -ī, m. (15)
nut, noun, nux, nuctis, f. (5)
on the ground, phrase, humi (9)
on, prep. w/abl., in (4)
one, adj., ūnus (15)
(to) order, verb, imperō, -āre, -āvī, -ātum (12)
out of, prep. w/abl., ē, ex (3)

P

(an) oval race course, noun, circus, -ī, m. (3)
over, prep. w/acc., super (9)
parent, noun, parens, parentis, m. or f. (Rv. 8)
party, noun, convīvium, -ī, n. (14)
paw, noun, pēs, pedis, m. (9)
peacock, noun, pāvo, pavōnis, m. (11)

(to) pile up, verb, cumulō, -āre, -āvī, -ātum (12)
pink, adj., roseus, -a, -um (14)
pity, noun, misericordia, -ae, f. (9)
play (on an instrument), verb, canō, -āre, -āvī, -ātum (8)
(to) play, verb, lūdo, lūdere, lūsī, lūsum (3)
please, sī placet (10)
(to) pluck, pick, verb, carpō, -ere, carpsī, carptum (5)
(to) pluck, verb, vellō, -ere, vellī, vulsum (11)
(to) polish, verb, līmo, -are, -avi, -atum (Rv. 14)
(to) praise, verb, laudō, -āre, -āvī, -ātum (8)
(to) prepare, verb, parō, -āre, -āvī, -ātum (8)
pretty, adj., bellus, -a, -um, adj. (14)
prize, noun, praemium, -ī, n. (3)
proud, adj., superbus, -a, -um (4)
proudly, adv., superbe (Rv. 14)

Q

queen, noun, rēgīna, -ae, f. (8)

R

rabit, noun, cunīculus, -ī m. (3)
(a) race, noun, curriculum, -ī, n. (3)
(to) read, verb, legō, -ere, lēgī, lectum (5)
(to) realize, verb, intellegō, -ere, -lexī, -lectum (12)
red, adj., ruber, rubra, rubrum (12)
referee, noun, **arbiter, arbitrī,** m.(3)
(to) repay, verb, reddō, -ere,-didi, -ditum (10)
(to) reserve, verb, reservō, -āre, -āvī, -ātum (8)
response, noun, responsum, -ī, n. (15)
road, noun, via, viae, f. (4)
(to) roar, verb, fremō, -ere, -uī, -itum (9)
(to) rob, verb, exspoliō, -āre (1)
rope, noun, fūnis, fūnis, m. (9)
rosy, adj., roseus, -a, -um (14)
(to) run, verb, curro, currere, cucurrī, cursum (3)
runner, noun, cursor, cursōris, m. (3)

S

sad, adj., maestus, -a, -um (10)
(he/she/it) said, verb, inquit (Rv. 15)
(to) save, verb, reservō, -āre, -āvī, -ātum (8)
(to) say, verb, narrō, -āre (1)
school, noun, lūdus, -ī, m. (2)
sea, noun, mare, -is, n. (10)
second, adj., secundus, -a, -um (16)
(to) see, verb, videō, -ēre, vīdī, visum

Glossary: English to Latin

(to) sell, *verb,* venditō, -āre, āvī, -ātum *(13)*
seven, *adj.,* septem *(15)*
seventh, *adj.,* septimus, -a, -um *(16)*
(to) shake, *verb,* quatiō, quatere, quassī, quassum *(14)*
sharp, *adj.,* acutus, -a, -um **(Rv. 9)**
sheep, *noun,* ovis, ovis, *f. (2)*
shell, *noun,* testa, -ae, *f. (4)*
shepherd, *noun,* **pastor, pastōris,** *m. (2)*
(to) shout, *verb,* clamō, -āre, -āvī, -ātum **(1)**
(to) show, *verb,* monstrō, -āre, -āvī, -ātum
(to) shut out, hatch, excludō, -ere, -clūsī, -clūsum
(to) sing, *verb,* cantō, -āre, -āvī, -ātum *(12)*
(to) sit, *verb,* sedeō, -ēre, sedī, sessum *(Rv. 12)*
six, *adj.,* sex *(15)*
sixth, *adj.,* sextus, -a, -um **(16)**
skin, *noun,* pellis, -is, *f. (10)*
sleep, *noun,* somnus, -ī, *m. (3)*
slipper, *noun,* calceus, -ī, *m. (14)*
slow, *adj.,* tardus, -a, -um *(3)*
(to) smile, *verb,* rīdeō, -ēre, rīsī, rīsum **(1)**
snowy, *adj.,* niveus, -a, -um *(7)*
soil, *noun,* humus, -ī, *f. (7)*
(to) spill, *verb,* effundō, -ere, -fūdī, -fūsum *(14)*
(to) stand, *verb,* stō, -āre, stetī, -ātum *(Rv. 6)*
storeroom, *noun,* cella, -ae, *f. (13)*
storm, *noun,* tempestās, -ātis, *f. (7)*
story teller, *noun,* narrātor, narrātōris, *m. (1)*
stream, *noun,* rīvus, -ī, *m. (11)*
student (boy), *noun,* discipulus, -ī, *m. (Rv.1)*
student (girl), *noun,* discupula, -ae, *f. (Rv.1)*
(to) study, *verb,* studeō, -ēre, -uī, --------
(to) subtract, *verb,* dedūcō, -ere, -duxī, -ductum *(15)*
summer, *noun,* aestās, aestātis, *f. (5)*
(to) swallow, *verb,* dēvorō, -āre, -āvī, -ātum *(1)*
(to) swear, *verb,* iūrō, -āre, -āvī, -ātum *(10)*
(to) swell up, *verb,* turgeō, -ēre, tursī, _____ *(Rv. 12)*
swift, *adj.,* citus, -a, -um *(Rv. 7)*
swiftly, *adv.,* cito *(6)*
table, *noun,* mensa, -ae, *f. (Rv. 15)*

teacher (female), *noun,* magistra, -ae, *f. (Rv. 2)*
teacher (male), *noun,* magister, magistrī, *m.*
(to) tell, *verb,* narrō, -āre *(1)*
ten, *adj.,* decem *(15)*
tenth, *adj.,* decimus, -a, -um *(16)*
terra, -ae, *f., noun,* ground, earth, land *(Rv. 12)*
then, *adv.,* tum *(12)*
third, *adj.,* tertius, -a, -um **(16)**
though, *prep. w/acc.,* per *(8)*
(a) thousand, *adj.,* mille *(15)*
three, *adj.,* trēs *(15)*
(to) throw, *verb,* iactō, -āre, -avi, -ātum *(9)*
time, *noun,* tempus, temporis, *n. (16)*
tired, *adj.,* defessus, -a, -um *(4)*
to, *prep. w/acc.,* ad **(2)**
tooth, *noun,* dens, dentis, *m. (6)*
tortoise, *noun,* testūdo, testūdinis, *f. (4)*
toward, *prep. w/acc.,* ad *(2)*
(to) track, *verb,* vestīgō, -āre, -āvī, -ātum **(10)**
tree, *noun,* arbor, arboris, *f. (4)*
truth, *noun,* vēritās, vēritātis, *f.(2)*
turtle, *noun,* testūdo, testudōnis, *f. (Rv. 6)*
two, *adj.,* duo *(15)*
ugly, *adj.,* foedus, -a, -um *(11)*
umpire, *noun,* **arbiter, arbitrī,** *m.(3)*
under, *prep. w/abl.,* sub **(4)**
understand, *verb,* intellegō, -ere, -lexī, -lectum *(12)*
(to) use, *verb,* ūtor *(4)*
vain, *adj.,* vānus, -a, -um *(11)*
(to) vanish, *verb,* evānesco, evānescere, evānuī, ------- *(14)*
village, *noun,* vīcus, -i, *m. (1)*
(to) visit, *verb,* visitō, -āre, -āvī, -ātum
(to) wait for, *verb,* exspecto, -āre, -āvī, -ātum *(3)*
(to) wake, *verb,* excitō, -āre, -āvī, -ātum *(4)*
(to) walk, *verb,* ambulō, -āre, -āvi, -ātum **(4)**
(to) wander, *verb,* errō, -āre, -āvī, -ātum *(8)*
(to) warn, *verb,* moneō, -ēre, -uī, -itum *(1)*
(to) was, *verb,* erat
(to) wash, *verb,* lavō, -āre, -āvī, -ātum *(11)*
(to) watch, *verb,* spectō, -āre, -āvī, -atum
(to) wear, *verb,* gestō, -āre, -āvī, -ātum *(11)*

Glossary: English to Latin

weary, *adj., defessus, -a, -um*
weather, *noun, tempestās, -ātis, f. (7)*
(to) well up, *verb, turgeō, -ēre, tursī,---------- (4)*
wheat, *noun, triticum, -i, n. (6)*
when, quando (16)
where, *adv., ubi (6)*
while, dum (10)
(to) whisper, *verb, insusurrō, -āre, -āvī, -ātum (6)*
white, *adj., albus, -a, -um (7)*
wife, *noun, uxor, uxoris, f. (6)*
(to) win, *verb, conciliō, -āre, -āvi, -ātum*
wind, *noun, ventus, -ī, m. (7)*
windy, *adj., ventōsus, -a, -um (7)*
wine, *noun, vīnum, -i, n. (6)*
winner, *noun, victor, victōris, m. (4)*
winter, *noun, hiems, hiēmis, f. (7)*
wisdom, *noun, sapientia, -ae, f. (8)*
wolf, *noun, lupus, -ī, m. (2)*
work, *noun, labor, laboris, f. (7)*
(to) work, *verb, laboro, -āre (2)*
world, *noun, mundus, -ī, m. (12)*
(to) write, *verb, scrībo, -ere, scripsī, scriptum (5)*
year, *noun, annus, -ī, m. (16)*
yellow, *adj., flāvus, -a, -um (7)*
young man, *noun, adulēscēns, adulēscentis, m. (14)*
young woman, *noun, virgo, virginis, f. (14)*

Index

Ablative of Place, 244
Ablative of Time, 283, 286
Adjectives, 61, 79, 125
Adverbs, 127, 139, 147
Cardinal Numbers One, Two & Three, 273, 285
Commands, 35, 86, 90, 111, 248, 258
Commands for Third Conjugation, 90
Conjugate Linking Verb, 157
Dative Case, 65
Demonstrative Pronoun as Adjective, 161, 212, 218 245, 246, 259
Demonstrative Pronoun Chant, 155, 161, 167, 176, 191, 199, 218, 237
First Conjugation 69, 121, 218, 219
Difference Between Present and Perfect Tense, 203
Forming Questions, 99, 97
Future Perfect Tense, 281
Genitive of Possession, 31
Linking Verb, 66, 95, 99, 157, 243, 258
Noun-Adjective Agreement, 78, 146,267
Perfect Tense, 194, 197, 277, 281
Personal Pronouns, 158, 163
Personal Pronouns Chant, 175
Pluperfect Tense, 229, 277
Possessive Adjective, 248, 249, 259, 272
Predicate Adjectives, 103
Prepositions, 173, 196, 280

Present Stem for Third Conjugation Verbs, 89
Present Verb Stem, 85, 89, 111
Relative Pronoun Chant, 265
Roman Numerals, 267
Second Conjugation, 69, 218, 219
Showing Emphasis, 158, 159
The Goose that Laid the Golden Egg, 287
The Grasshopper & the Ants, 141
The Lion & the Mouse, 179
The Milkmaid & Her Pail, 251
The Tortoise & the Hare, 73
The Town Mouse & the Country Mouse, 107
The Vain Jackdaw, 213
Third Conjugation Verbs, 47, 48, 53, 69, 89, 121, 203, 219
Third Declension Chant, 147
Third Declension I-Stem Nouns, 133, 137, 147, 148, 171
Third Declension Nouns, 27, 168
Third Declension Neuter, 168
Verb Stem, 18, 239
Verb Synopses 122, 131, 139, 145, 221, 232, 240, 257, 281, 282
Verb Tense, 17, 193, 227